The Education Fact File

SECOND EDITION

A handbook of education information in the UK

*June Statham and Donald Mackinnon
with Heather Cathcart and Margaret Hales
at the Open University*

HODDER AND STOUGHTON

LONDON   SYDNEY   AUCKLAND   TORONTO
in association with the Open University

British Library Cataloguing in Publication Data
The Education fact file.—2nd. ed.
  1. Great Britain. Education
  I. Statham, June
  370.941

  ISBN 0–340–54467–8

First published in Great Britain 1989
Second impression 1990
Second edition 1991

Typeset by Wearside Tradespools, Fulwell, Sunderland
Printed in Great Britain for Hodder and Stoughton Educational, a division of Hodder
and Stoughton Ltd, Mill Road, Dunton Green, Sevenoaks, Kent by Clays Ltd., St Ives plc.

The Education Fact File

CONTENTS

Introduction To The Second Edition

The Education Fact File has been produced primarily as a set book for the Open University second level course E208, *Exploring Educational Issues*. But it has been designed to stand independently of E208, and we hope it will also be found useful by people studying other education courses, in the Open University or elsewhere, and indeed by anyone interested in education, whether as parent, teacher, student or citizen.

As we emphasise throughout the book, we are living in a period of rapid and profound educational change — hence our second edition, only two years after the first. This book too will inevitably become outdated, and the authors and publishers hope to produce new, up-to-date, editions as the need arises. Accordingly, we would welcome any comments, criticisms, suggestions for inclusion, and above all corrections of mistakes.

Anyone who compares the two editions closely will find that our new figures do not always update the old in exactly the same form. Very occasionally, the old statistics are not updated at all. This is because many of our official sources alter from year to year the ways in which they collect or publish data, for reasons not always self-evident.

This is not a work of original research; almost all our information comes from published sources, mainly official publications, but also published academic research, and other reference books more specialised than this one. Our sources are acknowledged in the lists of 'Sources and further reading' at the end of each chapter. (If any source we have used has inadvertently been omitted, we apologise, and ask to be told so that proper acknowledgement can be made in future editions.) Numbers taken from these sources are usually 'rounded' in our diagrams. Occasionally this means that percentages add up to slightly more or less than 100. Dates are usually given as they appear in our sources. Where two years are mentioned (e.g. 1988–9), this refers to a single academic (or, where appropriate, a single financial) year; it does not mean the two calendar years (1988 and 1989). Where a single year (e.g. 1989) is given, this usually refers to the specific point in that calendar year when the information was collected.

In preparing the book, we have received a great deal of assistance from many individuals and institutions. We particularly thank Ann Floyd, the former Dean of the Open University School of Education, without whose support the project would not even have begun. We obtained financial assistance for the writing, editing and design of the book from the Open University's New Development Fund. The E208 Course Team, and especially Peter Woods, the Course Team Chair, were a constant source of help and advice. The resources of the libraries of the Open University and the London University Institute of Education were indispensable, and, as always, their staff were extremely knowledgeable and helpful. In preparing the book, we received invaluable assistance with our computers from John Close and David Graddol. Clive Newman, Jenny Hurstfield and G. D.

Jayalakshmi provided encouragement and support, and John Taylor, of the Open University Publishing Division, gave us expert guidance. The first edition was edited for publication by Andrew Coleman; we hope that some of his good influence on our style has survived into the second.

For suggestions as to what the book might contain, and for comments on various drafts, we are grateful to: W. R. Armstrong, Peter Barnes, Bob Bell, Kevin Brehony, Nick Brenton, Ben Cosin, Keri Davies, Rosemary Deem, Bernard Farr, Ross Fergusson, Mike Flude, Bob Glaister, Merril Hammer, Barbara Mayor, Ron McCartney, Ian McNay, Jenny Meegan, Dominic Newbould, Desmond Nuttall, Jenny Ozga, Nigel Pigott, Ali Rattansi, Philip Robinson, Joan Swann, Will Swann, Tony Travers, Leslie Wagner, Andy Wiggans and Martin Woodhead.

We have been able to follow most, though not all, of the suggestions for additions to or elaboration of the contents of the book. But of course responsibility for omissions and any remaining mistakes is ours.

The *Fact File* and the Open University

The *Education Fact File* has been especially prepared as part of an Open University degree course, E208 *Exploring Educational Issues*. The Open University has more than 130 such undergraduate courses, a wide range of self-contained study packs, and programmes of study for professional development. The School of Education in particular offers 12 undergraduate courses, advanced diplomas and an MA in Education; there is something of interest and value to teachers and non-teachers alike.

Exploring Educational Issues is a second-level undergraduate course: it consists of 32 correspondence 'units', 15 television programmes and six audio cassettes, together with two readers and this *Education Fact File*.

Exploring Educational Issues provides a general introduction to education in the United Kingdom today, covering the most recent developments and at the same time setting them in the context of perennial educational questions and principles. It made its first appearance in 1989, and it is kept up-to-date.

The issues explored include:

- parents and schools
- curriculum and assessment
- classroom learning
- school effectiveness
- control and finance of education
- 'race', gender and education
- education and the economy

The authors come from different academic disciplines, and the course is interdisciplinary in nature. It draws on psychology, sociology, economics, philosophy and history wherever these seem appropriate and useful.

Exploring Educational Issues is intended to be accessible to everyone interested in education — whether as teacher, student, parent, governor, or simply citizen. Its aim is to help and encourage its students to reach their own informed, reasoned conclusions about the major issues in education today.

For more information write to: Central Enquiry Service, The Open University, P.O. Box 71, Milton Keynes MK7 6AG.

CHAPTER 1   HOW TO USE THIS BOOK

The Education Fact File aims to provide basic factual information, in words, diagrams and numbers, about education in the United Kingdom today.

In Section One, we present some information about the social and historical background to current events and issues. Chapter 2 gives an outline of some social structures and processes that are important for education. Chapter 3 summarises the principal official reports on education and related subjects that have been prepared since the Education Act of 1944. And Chapter 4 outlines the most important educational legislation from the monumental Education Act of 1870 to what may prove of comparable significance, the Education Reform Act of 1988.

In Section Two, we describe the educational systems of the four countries that make up the United Kingdom. The principal educational institutions are outlined in Chapter 5; the ways in which they are organised and controlled are explained in Chapter 6. Chapter 7 looks at the educational professionals who work in various ways within the systems. Chapter 8 outlines the newly introduced procedures of educational finance and resources — where the money comes from, and where it goes. Finally, Chapter 9 summarises the main qualifications available at every level within (and outside) the education systems.

Section Three covers a variety of processes occurring within these education systems. Chapter 10 looks at the school curriculum and its assessment, after the 1988 Act. Chapter 11 provides information about a set of issues that have long been at the centre of educational debate and controversy — educational attainment, and its relationship to equality and inequality between children from different groups and categories. And Chapter 12 summarises the position today of young people just over school-leaving age: the new problems they face, the new possibilities open to them.

Section Four has just two chapters, both in the form of alphabetical lists: Chapter 13 is a glossary of important educational terms, and Chapter 14 deciphers some of the most widespread educational acronyms and abbreviations. For ease of reference, both chapters include some words and abbreviations that are treated more fully in other chapters, as well as many that are not covered elsewhere in the book.

Facts and figures

All these chapters are intended to be *factual*, to tell the reader what the educational world is like, not to give the interpretations or judgements — and certainly not the prejudices — of the authors or anyone else. This is a worthwhile aim, we believe, but one impossible to fulfil. Although we have done our best to fulfil it, we must offer some words of caution about taking the contents of this book as facts, let alone *the* facts about education.

First, and most obviously, the book is bound to contain errors. Some of these may come from our sources; others, alas, will be all our own work. We hope that these are few and trivial, but we are resigned to accepting that a book of this character will have some.

Secondly, we have inevitably made choices about which facts to include, and which to leave out. Sometimes these have been slightly forced choices, because of gaps and limitations in the available data. But much more often, we have had to decide what we considered most significant and telling from an embarrassment of information. This is where interpretation is unavoidable, and prejudice a very real danger. We cannot, of course, claim to be unprejudiced; people are not normally aware of their own prejudices. What we can and do say is that we have never knowingly excluded or modified any information in order to favour our own beliefs, values or political preferences.

Thirdly, even the categories in which data are presented depend on controversial judgements, and are open to unintended distortion. There are different ways of defining 'social class', for example, or of identifying ethnic groups, and these can lead to very different pictures of the class structure or ethnic composition of the country, and of the relationship between class or ethnicity and, say, educational attainment. The particular cases of social class and ethnic group are discussed in Chapter 11; here we want to make the general point that choosing categories for presenting 'the facts' is fraught with uncertainty and controversy.

Finally, we would like to warn against leaping too quickly to what may seem obvious interpretations of facts and their relationships, such as conclusions about cause and effect. Above all, we should be cautious about accepting plausible interpretations of one fact or set of facts in isolation, without at least checking that our interpretation fits in with other relevant information.

Reading and referring

One of the first things we had to decide in preparing this book was whether it was to be primarily a reference book, to be consulted as required for some particular piece of information, or a genuine text, to be read through from beginning to end. As you will see, it has ended up as something of both. Four of the chapters are really elaborated lists: Chapters 3 and 4 present their reports and Acts in chronological order; Chapters 13 and 14 list their terms and acronyms in alphabetical order. We do not expect many people to read their way through these chapters; on the other hand, if you want to look up the main provisions of, say, the 1987 Teachers' Pay and Conditions Act, or distinguish GIST from GRIST, you will find the information easily accessible there.

The other chapters, though, *are* designed to be read through as well as referred to. They deal with subject matter that does not so readily lend itself to division into self-contained entries. We hope that each chapter provides a clear and straightforward introduction to the basic facts and figures in the area it covers. The inevitable disadvantage is that it is not quite so easy to look things up in these chapters as it would be in a list. Besides, many topics do not fit neatly into one and only one chapter or section, however carefully these are devised. But the book has a comprehensive index, and cross-references within and between chapters. With judicious use of these, we hope, you should not have great difficulty in finding out what you want to know.

Scope

The book covers the whole of the United Kingdom — England, Scotland, Wales (which together form Great Britain) and Northern Ireland. (It does not cover the Isle of Man or the Channel Islands; they are not part of the United Kingdom, but Crown dependencies, with their own governments.) However, its coverage of these countries is far from equal. England, or for many purposes England and Wales together, receives much the most attention. Whether this is justified is open to argument; we are far from certain that we have always got the balance right. England is, of course, by far the biggest country in the United Kingdom, with 83% of its population (England and Wales together have 88%) (see Chapter 2, Figure 2.1). By virtue of its size, developments in English education usually exert greater influence on the other countries than theirs do on England. And a practical point: detailed data on English education are usually easier to find. We have tried to use United Kingdom data whenever we could, but often we have had to illustrate particular points from English, or English and Welsh, figures. We hope this does not mislead; we always try to make clear what countries or regions our figures cover.

Of course there are differences between the countries in the structure of their education systems, and in the processes within them. Northern Ireland, for example, still has its grammar schools, whereas maintained schools in England, Scotland and Wales are now almost entirely comprehensive. Scotland has its own system of examinations, both in schools and in vocational education; England, Wales and Northern Ireland share a common system. And so on. Differences in structure are spelled out in the appropriate chapters, and where we judge there to be significant differences in educational processes from country to country, we have pointed them out.

Change

Finally, we are only too well aware that we have produced this book during what promises to be a period of the most profound, widespread and rapid educational change for many years — mainly, but not only, as a consequence of the 1988 Education Reform Act. The processes of change are well under way, but still far from complete, as the second edition goes to press (late 1990). In almost every chapter, we have had to point forward to what seem to be the likeliest important developments in the near future, as well as describing things as they are now. The sudden resignation of Mrs Thatcher while the book is in press almost certainly heralds further, unpredictable changes.

4

CHAPTER 2   SOCIAL BACKGROUND

Social factors of fundamental importance for the education system include the size of the population, its structure by age and sex, its distribution across nations and regions, its composition by social class and ethnic group and — not least — the ways in which any of these change from year to year.

Population

The United Kingdom has a total population of about 57 million, divided unevenly among its four constituent countries as shown in Figure 2.1.

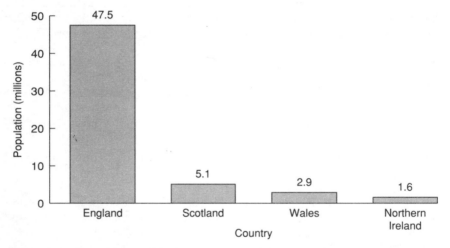

Figure 2.1   Populations of the four countries of the United Kingdom, 1988 (Adapted from OPCS, 1989c, Table B)

England is divided, for some official statistics, into eight standard regions. As Figure 2.2 shows, three of these are greater in population than Scotland, seven greater than Wales, and all eight greater than Northern Ireland. By far the largest is the South East, with 17.3 million; of these, about 6.7 million live in Greater London alone, which is thus more populous than any of the other regions of England, or any of the other countries of the United Kingdom.

Figure 2.3 gives, for the United Kingdom as a whole, the numbers of males and females in each of five age groups below the age of 25. These are the people most likely to be, now or in the very near future, full-time pupils or students in educational institutions.

The size of the population of school or college age has important

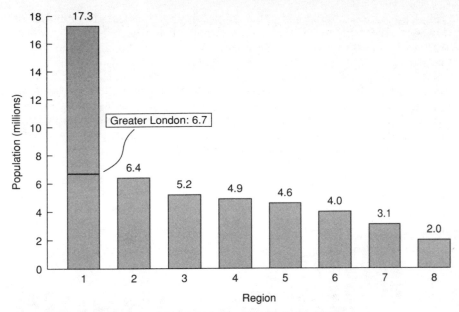

Figure 2.2   Populations of the eight regions of England, 1988
(Adapted from OPCS, 1989c, Table B)
Key to regions: 1 South East; 2 North West; 3 West Midlands; 4 Yorkshire and
Humberside; 5 South West; 6 East Midlands; 7 North; 8 East Anglia

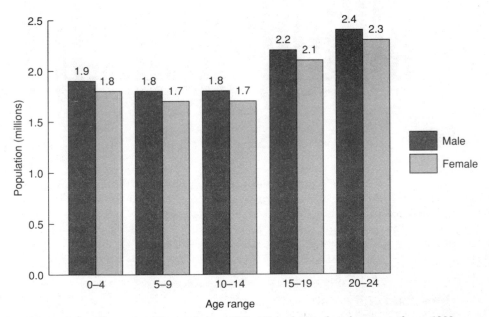

Figure 2.3   The under-25 population of the United Kingdom by age and sex, 1988
(Adapted from OPCS, 1989c, Table 6; Government Statistical Service, 1989,
Table 1)

implications for educational policy and planning. It affects the number of schools (see Chapter 5) and the number of teachers (see Chapter 7) required, and therefore affects the amount of expenditure needed by the education system (see Chapter 8). Changes from year to year in the number of people in each age group create difficulties for planning, especially as birth rates are notoriously difficult to predict; estimating what the school population will be in more than five years' time becomes increasingly speculative and uncertain. Figure 2.4 shows how the number of births in the United Kingdom has varied from year to year since 1964, when it reached its highest figure since the 1920s.

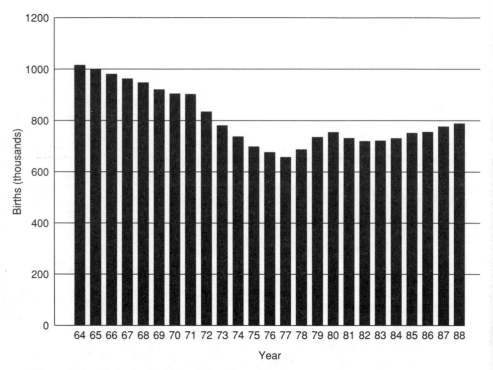

Figure 2.4   Births in the United Kingdom, 1964–88
(Adapted from CSO, 1982, Table 2.24; CSO, 1989a, Table 2.16; OPCS, 1989c, Table 8)

The United Kingdom's population grew steadily from the end of World War II until the early 1970s, since when its total has remained stable. But the *age structure* within this total has changed, in the 1970s and 1980s, towards fewer younger and more older people. In 1988, 19% of the population were under 15 (compared with 24% in 1971), and 16% were over 65 (compared with 13% in 1971) (CSO, 1990, Table 2.2).

Household and family

About a third of all households in Great Britain have at least one dependent child. Of these children, 84% live with an adult couple, and

16% with a lone parent (15% with a mother, 1% with a father) (OPCS, 1989a, Figure 2).

The great majority of families are small: over 80% of households in Great Britain with dependent children have either one or two children (but see Figure 2.15 below). Figure 2.5 shows the numbers of households in the mid-1980s with various numbers of children.

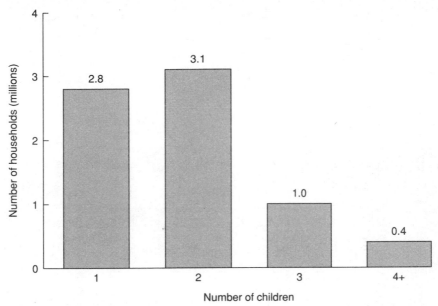

Figure 2.5   Numbers of households with various numbers of dependent children aged under 19, Great Britain 1984
(Adapted from OPCS, 1985)

Since World War II, births outside marriage have increased by five times as a percentage of all births in the United Kingdom, from 5% (1951) to 25% (1988). During the same period, divorces have also increased: in England and Wales the increase was more than fourfold, from 0.3% to 1.3% of the married population per annum (CSO, 1987b, Table A.1; OPCS, 1989a, Tables 8 and 14).

Men are more likely than women to be 'economically active', that is, in effect, to be in or seeking paid employment outside the home (see Figure 2.8), but this difference is decreasing with time (see Figure 2.9). Women with dependent children are less likely to have full-time jobs but more likely to have part-time jobs, than women without. The younger her youngest child is, the less likely a mother is to have any employment, full- or part-time, as Figure 2.6 shows.

Social class and occupation

The terms 'working class' and 'middle class' are in almost universal use, but under many different definitions and interpretations, which can lead to

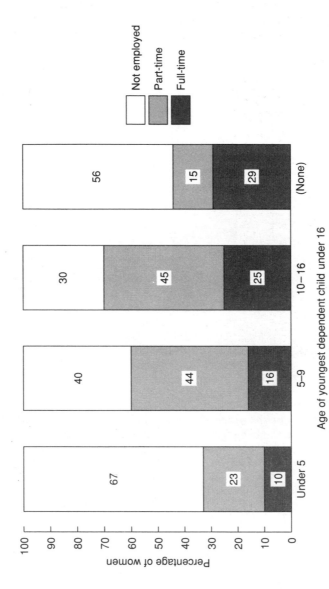

Figure 2.6   Percentages of women in employment, by age of youngest dependent child under 16 (Adapted from CSO, 1989, Table 4.7)

different pictures of the class structure of the country. One way of obtaining figures for the classes is to ask people what class they think they belong to. When asked their social class, about 70% of people in Great Britain identify themselves as working (or 'upper working') class, and about 25% as middle class. (Slightly more identify their parents as working class, and fewer identify their parents as middle class.) Figure 2.7 gives more detail about 'self-rated' social class in the mid-1980s.

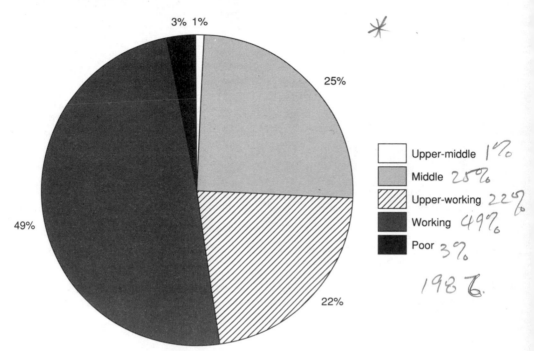

3% 1%

25%

49%

22%

Upper-middle 1%

Middle 25%

Upper-working 22%

Working 49%

Poor 3%

1986.

Figure 2.7   Self-rated social class, Great Britain 1986
(Adapted from CSO, 1987b, Table A.6)

But demographers and social scientists also use more objective measures. The most common practice in educational research is to take *occupation* as the basis for identifying class, often adopting one of the official classifications of occupations used by the Office of Population Censuses and Surveys (OPCS) — socioeconomic classes, socioeconomic groups or, most usually, the one actually called social classes, which is currently:

I   Professional (this includes university teachers)
II   Intermediate (this includes school teachers)
III(N)   Skilled non-manual
III(M)   Skilled manual
IV   Partly skilled
V   Unskilled

Figure 2.8 shows the numbers of men and women in Great Britain at the time of the 1981 Census who were employed in the various OPCS social classes or out of employment.

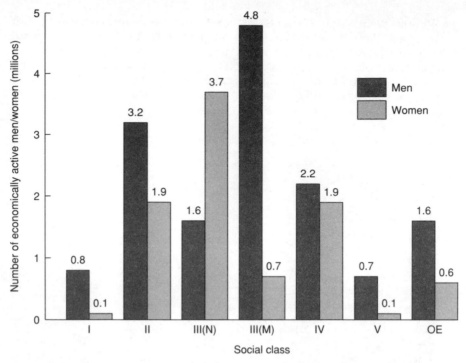

Figure 2.8   Numbers of economically active men and women in each social class or out of employment, Great Britain 1981
(Adapted from OPCS, 1984, Tables i and 18A)
Note: These figures are based on the analysis of a 10% sample of census returns; the retired, temporarily sick, students and members of the armed forces are excluded; 'OE' refers to the category 'out of employment'

In practice, most educational researchers studying social class have used simplified or compressed versions of the OPCS classification. Frequently, classes I, II and III(N) are taken to be middle class, and III(M), IV and V to be working class. Children are generally classified according to their fathers' occupations. For Great Britain as a whole, according to the 1981 Census, this makes about 49% of the population middle class and 51% working class. But there are substantial variations from country to country and region to region. Scotland and Wales, and the North, North West, Yorkshire and Humberside, West Midlands, East Midlands and East Anglia regions of England have a lower percentage of their population in classes I, II and III(N) and a higher percentage in III(M), IV and V than Great Britain as a whole, whereas the South West and especially the South East have a higher percentage in I, II and III(N) and a lower percentage in III(M), IV and V than the British average. (The extremes are the North, with 42% in classes I, II and III(N), and the South East with 56% (OPCS, 1984, Tables 1, 17 and 18A.)

Unemployment shows a similar geographical pattern, being above the United Kingdom average (of 8% in 1988) in Northern Ireland (16.4%), the North of England (11.9%), Scotland (11.2%), the North West of England

(10.7%) and Wales (10.5%), and below average in the South East (5.2%), South West (6.3%) and East Midlands (7.2%) of England (CSO, 1989b, Table 10.17).

As Figure 2.8 shows, substantially more men than women are economically active. However, differences between the sexes in economic activity have diminished over the years. This is illustrated in Figure 2.9.

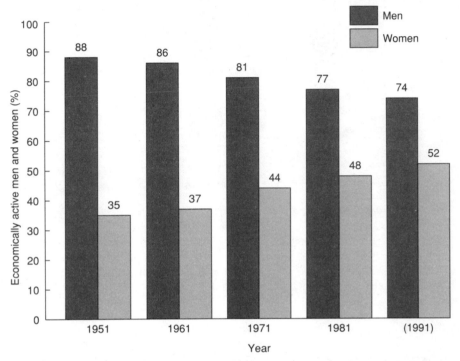

Figure 2.9 Percentages of men and women over school-leaving age who are economically active, United Kingdom 1951–91
(Adapted from CSO, 1989a, Table 4.5)
Note: The 1991 figures are estimates

One of the most influential categorisations of social class, other than those of the OPCS, has been that used by the Oxford Social Mobility Study. It, too, is based on a detailed classification of occupations (similar, though not identical, to those of the OPCS), which are grouped for many purposes into three social classes:

1 *Service class* or *salariat* (professional, managerial, etc.; this includes teachers)
2 *Intermediate class* (routine non-manual, small proprietors, etc.)
3 *Working class* (manual workers and supervisors of manual workers)
                                              (Goldthorpe and Hope, 1974)

By this classification, the social class distributions of the male population (women were not included in the Oxford study) of England and Wales in

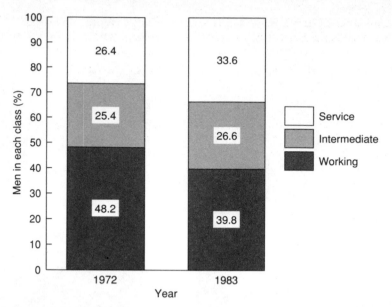

Figure 2.10   Percentages of male population in each social class, England and Wales 1972 and 1983
(Adapted from Goldthorpe and Payne, 1986, Table 6, 'new schema')

1972 and 1983 were as shown in Figure 2.10). The working class has declined as a percentage of the population. The intermediate and (especially) the service classes have increased.

Ethnic groups

Unlike age, sex and social class, ethnicity as such has not been used as a census category (though the OPCS plans to use it in the 1991 Census). The information in this section comes from sample surveys or from inference based on other census questions (notably about the country of birth of 'heads of household') and cannot be considered entirely reliable.

The OPCS warns that its own Labour Force Surveys, probably the main source of information about ethnic minority populations, are 'subject to relatively high sampling error' in this field (OPCS, 1985, p. 1). And figures for the country of birth of heads of household give only a rough estimate of ethnic minority populations, as some members of ethnic minorities live in households whose head was born in the United Kingdom, and some of those living in households whose head was born outside the United Kingdom do not belong to ethnic minorities.

A further source of uncertainty is that there is no single set of terms in use among researchers and census-takers for the different ethnic groups. Sometimes differences in terminology are merely the use of different words for the same or similar groups (such as 'West Indian' and 'Afro-Caribbean'); at other times, different sets of terms refer to different classifications and different ways of classifying. For example, a classification may be based on skin-colour, as in the OPCS Labour Survey's *White* and *Non-white*; or on country of origin or descent, as in the Rampton and Swann Reports' *West Indian*, *Asian* and *Other*; or on a mixture of both, as in Eggleston *et al.*'s (1986) *Afro-Caribbean*, *Asian* and *White*; or on country of birth of the head of household (as in the 1981 Census), with such categories of country as *the New Commonwealth and Pakistan*. Many terminological usages are controversial, and probably none is without its drawbacks. Here we adopt the categories used by our sources of data in each case. (The only exception is that instead of 'the New Commonwealth and Pakistan', we say simply 'the New Commonwealth'. Pakistan rejoined the Commonwealth in 1989, after most of the research reported here was published.)

By the OPCS categories, 95.5% of the population of Great Britain are white, while 4.5% belong to ethnic minority groups. The latter are concentrated in particular areas of the country. Two-thirds of all members of ethnic minority groups live in the former metropolitan counties of Greater London, West Midlands, West Yorkshire and Greater Manchester (compared with a quarter of the population as a whole). 41% of the 'non-white' population live in Greater London alone (compared with 12% of the population as a whole). By contrast, the regions of the North, East Anglia and the South West, plus the whole of Scotland and Wales, added together, contain 8% of the non-white population of Great Britain (compared with 32% of the population as a whole) (1985–7 figures: CSO, 1989b, Table 4.14).

This distribution leads to a very different ethnic composition of the population in different areas of the country. For example, a third of the population of the London Borough of Brent has a head of household born in the New Commonwealth, as does a quarter of the London Borough of

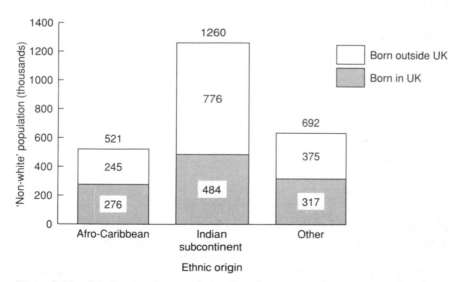

Figure 2.11   Ethnic minority population by ethnic origin, Great Britain 1985–7 (Adapted from OPCS, 1988, p. 30, Table 2)

Ealing, and a fifth of Leicester and of Slough. By contrast, virtually none of the population of many rural areas was born in the New Commonwealth (Commission for Racial Equality, 1985).

The 'non-white' population of Britain is made up of many different groups, some of whose members are immigrants, while others were born in Britain; this is illustrated with numbers from some of the main categories in Figure 2.11.

The largest of these groups, those born in or descended from those born in the Indian subcontinent, is itself divisible into sub-groups with important differences between them — such as language and religion. One obvious division is by the independent nations that make up the subcontinent; the major three are shown in Figure 2.12.

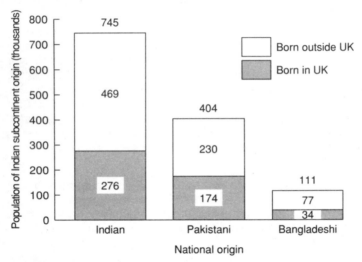

Figure 2.12   Population of Indian subcontinent origin or descent, Great Britain 1985–7
(Adapted from OPCS, 1988, p. 30)

Only a minority of immigrants to the United Kingdom have come from the New Commonwealth, and this minority has decreased in absolute terms, and even more in proportional terms, since the mid-1960s.

In 1965, there were about 206,000 immigrants to the United Kingdom, of whom 78,000 (38%) were from the New Commonwealth. In 1975, the total was 197,000, and the New Commonwealth figure was 66,000 (34%). By 1988, the total immigration figure had risen to 216,000, and the figure for the New Commonwealth had fallen to 50,000 (23%).

During most of the same period, there has been more emigration from the United Kingdom than immigration to it. Thus in 1965, there were about 284,000 emigrants (compared with 206,000 immigrants), and in 1975 there were 238,000 emigrants (compared with 197,000 immigrants). For a few years in the mid-1980s this pattern was reversed, and the number of people leaving the United Kingdom fell below the number entering. In 1985, for example, there were 174,000 emigrants (compared with 232,000 immigrants). But by the end of the decade, the old pattern had returned, and 1988 saw 237,000 emigrants (compared with 216,000 immigrants).

The overall picture of migration to and from the United Kingdom since 1965 is summarised in Figure 2.13: net immigration is shown as 'positive' migration (above the horizontal axis), and net emigration as 'negative' migration (below the axis).

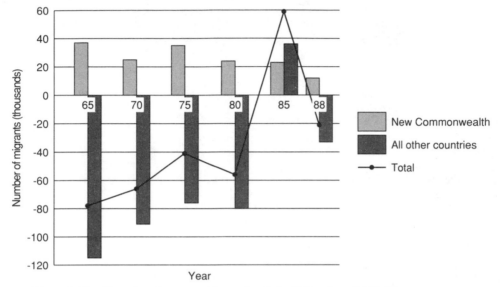

Figure 2.13   Net migration to and from the United Kingdom, 1965–88 (Adapted from OPCS, 1986, p. 37, Table 1; 1989c, Table 16)

With the passage of time, the proportion of the non-white population who were born in Great Britain is increasing. Thus, in the early 1980s, 86% of the non-white population aged under 16 were born in Britain compared with 14% born overseas; this is the exact reverse of the figures for those over 16, of whom 14% were born in Britain and 86% overseas (OPCS, 1986, p. 20, Table 4).

The non-white population is young; in 1985–7, 35% were aged under 16 and 18% aged 45 or over (compared with 20% under 16 and 36% 45 or over in the population as a whole) (OPCS, 1988, p. 31, Table 3).

As well as age differences, ethnic groups also show differences in their occupational structure and family patterns. Figure 2.14 shows occupational structures for Afro-Caribbean, Asian and white groups, using fathers' occupations as a basis.

There are differences between ethnic groups in the size of families, as is illustrated in Figure 2.15. The percentages are of all households in each ethnic group with dependent children under the age of 19.

There are also differences between ethnic groups in the percentage of one-parent families, as Figure 2.16 shows.

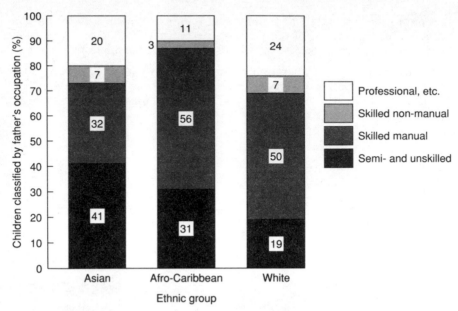

Figure 2.14   Percentages of Asian, Afro-Caribbean and white children with fathers in different occupational categories
(Adapted from Eggleston et al., 1986, Table 13)

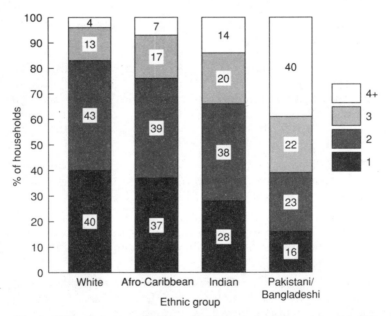

Figure 2.15   Percentages of households in each ethnic group with different numbers of dependent children
(Adapted from OPCS, 1985, Table 12)

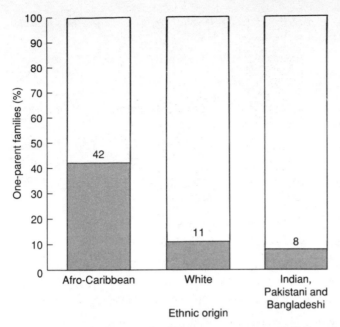

Figure 2.16   One-parent families as percentages of all households with dependent children in each ethnic group, Great Britain 1985–7 (Adapted from OPCS, 1989b, p. 13, Table 3)

Sources and further reading

CSO (1982) *Annual Abstract of Statistics*, No. 118; London, HMSO.

CSO (1987a) *Regional Trends*, No. 22, London, HMSO.

CSO (1987b) *Social Trends*, No. 17, London, HMSO.

CSO (1988a) *Annual Abstract of Statistics*, No. 124, London, HMSO.

CSO (1988b) *Social Trends*, No. 18, London, HMSO.

CSO (1989a) *Annual Abstract of Statistics*, No. 125, London, HMSO.

CSO (1989b) *Regional Trends*, No. 24, London, HMSO.

CSO (1990) *Monthly Digest of Statistics*, No. 529, January 1990, London, HMSO.

Commission for Racial Equality (1985) *Ethnic Minorities in Britain: Statistical Information on the Pattern of Settlement*, London, Commission for Racial Equality.

Eggleston, J., Dunn, D., Anjali, M. and Wright, C. (1986) *Education for Some: The Educational and Vocational Experiences of 15–18-year-old Members of Minority Ethnic Groups*, Stoke-on-Trent, Trentham Books.

Goldthorpe, J. H. and Hope, K. (1974) *The Social Grading of Occupations*, Oxford, Clarendon Press.

Goldthorpe, J. H. and Payne, C. (1986) Trends in intergenerational social mobility in England and Wales 1972–1983, *Sociology*, Vol. 20, No. 1, pp. 1–24.

Government Statistical Service (1989) *Educational Statistics for the United Kingdom: 1989 Edition*, London, HMSO.

OPCS (1984) *Census 1981: Economic Activity in Great Britain*, London, HMSO.

OPCS (1985) *OPCS Monitor LFS85/1 (Labour Force Survey 1984)*, London, Office of Population Censuses and Surveys.

OPCS (1986) *Population Trends*, No. 46, London, HMSO.

OPCS (1988) *Population Trends*, No. 54, London, HMSO.

OPCS (1989a) *OPCS Monitor 5589/1*, London, Office of Population Censuses and Surveys.

OPCS (1989b) *Population Trends*, No. 57, London, HMSO.

OPCS (1989c) *Population Trends*, No. 58, London, HMSO.

CHAPTER 3 OFFICIAL REPORTS

This chapter contains summaries of the principal findings and recommendations of some of the major official reports on education and related topics from 1944 until the present day. Inevitably, not all reports can be covered, and the summaries of those included are brief and highly selective. (See the 'Sources and further reading' section at the end of this chapter.)

Almost all of these reports were prepared by committees of inquiry appointed directly by government ministers (though we have also included a small number of particularly important reports produced by working parties or study groups attached to government ministries). All recent committees of inquiry, and some in the past, have been set up specifically for the task in hand, but between 1944 and 1967 many of the inquiries were undertaken by the Central Advisory Councils for Education (CACE) for England and for Wales, bodies set up under the 1944 Education Act to advise ministers on important educational issues. The reports are usually best known by the name of the committee's chairperson — 'The Plowden Report', 'The Warnock Report' and so on.

Where reports have led to legislation (see also Chapter 4), or were otherwise very influential, we have tried to indicate this. In some cases, though, reports seem to have had little impact, and in many others their effects are difficult to assess.

Unless otherwise indicated, the reports apply to England and Wales.

1944 Fleming — Public Schools and the General Education System

The committee that produced this report was set up to consider how public schools (defined as those belonging to the Headmasters' Conference or the Governing Bodies Association, together with 'comparable schools for girls') could develop and extend their association with the general education system. The report recommended that public schools should progressively be integrated into the state system by taking pupils who would be given state grants. To begin with, it was suggested, they should allocate a quarter of their places to this scheme, but eventually all their places should be open to pupils with state grants. [Though well received by the public schools, the scheme never came into effect, mainly because of the unwillingness of either central government or LEAs to take responsibility for payment of the grants.]

1944 McNair — Teachers and Youth Leaders

This report was concerned with the supply, recruitment and training of teachers (and youth leaders). It recommended (for both) increases in salary, and the extension of training courses to three years' full-time study.

1945   Percy — Higher Technological Education

This report investigated the needs of higher technological education in England and Wales, and the role of universities and technical colleges in meeting them. It recommended expansion of universities' science teaching and the creation of colleges of advanced technology. In addition, it recommended the establishment of organisations to co-ordinate the work of universities, colleges of technology and technical colleges at both local and national levels.

1946   Barlow — Scientific Manpower (Cmd. 6824)

This report argued that more university places were needed, especially for science students. [More places were provided.]

1947   Clarke — School and Life (CACE England)

This was the first CACE report. It examined 'the transition from school to independent life'. The committee interpreted its brief very widely, embracing all levels of education. Greatly increased expenditure was called for, particularly to reduce pupil/teacher ratios and improve unhealthy and unsuitable school buildings. Recommendations were made about a wide range of topics: relationships between school, home and neighbourhood; youth clubs and voluntary organisations; the health of children at school and young people at work; and 'compensatory' further education for workers in routine jobs. The main conclusion about education and employment was that purely educational aims came first: schools should not prepare pupils for particular types of employment; industry itself benefited from the teaching and learning of basic educational skills.

1948   Clarke — Out of School (CACE England)

Following up some of the conclusions of the first CACE report (see 1947 Clarke) this inquiry considered 'the natural interests and pursuits of school children out of school hours'. It urged that LEAs increase and improve facilities for children's play and recreation outside school hours, and that the government give financial support to voluntary bodies serving the out-of-school interests of school children. It further recommended that LEAs provide training courses for parents and all those who work with children.

1949   Evans/Aaron — The Future of Secondary Education in Wales (CACE Wales)

The report from this investigation made detailed recommendations for the organisation and curriculum of secondary education in Wales under the 1944 Education Act, and its relationship with primary and further education. It argued that education should be child-centred; it could take the form of either 'multilateral' schools or a dual system of grammar/technical schools and modern/technical schools (rather than a tripartite system), but must take into account variation in ability and aptitude between children. It recommended that the curriculum should emphasise free creation and co-operative inventiveness rather than passive assimilation, and that the study of history, geography and literature should give a central place to Wales. Particular attention was given to two issues: the rural and sparsely populated character of much of Wales, and the problems caused by the prevalence in Wales of two languages. As regards the latter, the committee recommended concentration on the pupil's first language, be it Welsh or English, with emphasis on conversation and oral work, but with a due subordinate place for written work. It argued that English must be taught well in predominantly Welsh-speaking areas, and that Welsh should be available as an option for all children in predominantly English-speaking areas.

1954   Gurney-Dixon — Early Leaving (CACE England)

This committee considered the factors influencing the age at which pupils left 'secondary schools which provide courses beyond the minimum school leaving age' — in practice, grammar schools. Research was commissioned, with data being gathered principally from a 10% sample of all grammar schools, whose headmasters supplied details of the 'background, school record and potentialities' of the 1946 intake. The report concluded that a pupil's performance was closely related to his or her father's occupational status: the higher that status, the better a pupil's performance, not only in leaving school less early but in having a better academic record and, in the headmaster's judgement, more 'promise'. These differences increased during secondary education: children from lower-status occupational groups declined from their 11 plus position relative to higher groups. The report offered some speculative explanations of these differences, most involving aspects of home background, including shortage of money, 'bad living conditions', and lack of educational experience and unfavourable attitudes to education among parents in the lower-status occupational groups. This was the first major investigation of the working of the 1944 Education Act (see Chapter 4), and it cast doubt on the effectiveness of the Act in reducing social-class-based inequalities in education. It recommended that more grammar school places be provided, and that financial provision be improved for pupils who remained at school after the minimum leaving age.

1955   Underwood — Maladjusted Children

The term 'maladjusted children' entered common usage after the 1944 Education Act, and it was the aim of this committee to investigate the education of such children. Recommendations included the use of day, rather than boarding, schools wherever possible; the setting up of a comprehensive Child Guidance Service in every LEA, with a strengthened role for educational psychologists; and the introduction of preventive measures such as increased nursery provision.

1959   Crowther — 15 to 18 (CACE England)

The Crowther committee was set up to consider the education of boys and girls between the ages of 15 and 18, and it was specifically asked to make recommendations about the place therein of exams below GCE level. The extensive research that was commissioned confirmed earlier findings (see 1954 Gurney-Dixon) about the relationship between fathers' occupational status and pupils' educational attainment. The higher the father's status, the greater the child's chance of attending a grammar rather than a secondary modern school, though the occupational group 'skilled manual workers' was so large that their children were by far the largest single group in all types of school. It was argued that there was considerable 'wastage' of talent, and much attention was paid to the 'neglected educational territory' of pupils who left school at 15 to follow a craft or technical, rather than an academic, career. The report recommended that there should be more further education. For 16–18-year-olds, half should be in full-time further education by 1979, compared with 12% at the time of the report. [In the event, major expansion in further education came slightly later, in the 1980s, with high unemployment of school leavers and such schemes as YTS.] It accepted that some comprehensive schools could be set up, but on the whole endorsed the existing tripartite system, and indeed suggested further divisions within it (and within further education). The report argued that, in secondary modern schools, the top third of pupils were capable of taking and benefiting from external exams below GCE level [the future CSE, first examined in 1965], but that the majority of pupils there should be spared them. It was also recommended that early subject specialisation should be discouraged (although study in depth was still desirable in the sixth form); and that two clauses from the 1944 Act which affected older pupils should be implemented, namely the raising of the school leaving age to 16 and compulsory part-time further education in county colleges. [The school leaving age was eventually raised, in 1972, but compulsory part-time further education has not been introduced.]

1960   Albermarle — The Youth Service in England and Wales

This committee was set up to review the Youth Service, which was thought to be demoralised and unprepared to deal with the increasing demand from the 'baby boom' children who were reaching adolescence. It recommended better training and status for youth leaders, a building programme of new premises and facilities, and the setting up of a Youth Service Development Council. It supported the continuation of a mixture of statutory and voluntary provision. [Most of the recommendations were implemented: the Development Council was set up to advise on a ten-year development programme; a large amount of building work was authorised and a special college opened in Leicester to train youth leaders, whose numbers doubled by 1966.]

1963   Newsom — Half Our Future (CACE England)

This investigation considered the education of pupils between 13 and 16 of average and less than average ability. The terms of reference show some overlap with those of the Crowther Committee; there was considerable overlap in the pool of CACE research on which the two committees drew, and some similarity in the recommendations offered (see 1959 Crowther). Like Crowther, Newsom accepted the tripartite system, believing there to be different levels of natural ability in children which could best be catered for by different kinds of school. But it did not accept that schools for the less able should be poorer in buildings, quality of teaching, or any other respect. It recommended maintenance of existing structures, but with a redistribution of spending to the benefit of the less able (for example, the rebuilding of inadequate secondary modern schools in slum areas). Again like Crowther, it strongly recommended the raising of the school leaving age to 16 [this eventually happened in 1972] and the provision of a more stimulating and demanding curriculum so that pupils had a wider choice of courses, including some 'broadly related to occupational interests', and others concerned with personal and social development, and 'imaginative experience through the arts'. It advised that all 16-year-old school leavers should be provided with some form of 'internal leaving certificate' containing a 'general school record'. [In practice, the curriculum for many less-able and average pupils became geared towards the new external CSE exam, contrary to Newsom's explicit recommendation. Only in the late 1970s did many schools begin to use pupil profiles and records of achievement similar to what Newsom had recommended.] Other miscellaneous recommendations were offered, including the provision of adequate religious instruction and positive guidance on sexual behaviour, the extension of the school day for older pupils, and the establishment of an experimental building programme 'to try out different forms of school organisation and teaching methods in buildings designed for the purpose'.

1963–4   Robbins — Higher Education (Cmnd. 2154)

Appointed to review the pattern of full-time higher education in Great Britain, and advise on its long-term development, this committee commissioned extensive new research and examination of existing research. Looking particularly at entry into higher education, it found, like previous reports (see 1954 Gurney-Dixon, 1959 Crowther, 1963 Newsom), a high correlation between social class and educational achievement. (At the extremes, a child of professional parents was about 20 times more likely than a child of semi-skilled and unskilled workers to enter full-time higher education.) Even with controls for measured intelligence, the correlation remained high. The *proportions* of children from each class entering higher education remained much as in the 1920s, although the *absolute numbers* had increased steadily with the expansion of educational provision. However, social class influence on attainment seemed to cease with university entry: once admitted, working-class students performed as well as middle-class students. Robbins concluded that there was a huge, untapped, and indeed often unsuspected, 'pool of ability' in the population, especially in lower socioeconomic groups. It recommended a massive expansion in higher education (from 216,000 places in 1962–3 to 390,000 in 1972–3 and 560,000 by 1980). Also recommended were: the establishment of the Council for National Academic Awards (CNAA) to grant degrees to students in non-university establishments [this happened the following year]; the raising of the status of teacher training colleges to colleges of education offering BEd degrees, and their integration into universities [the former has happened, but not the latter]; the granting of university status to the ten colleges of advanced technology [this was accepted], and in due course to other colleges [this did not happen; instead, from 1966 many of these became the new polytechnics]; and the establishment of special institutions for scientific and technological education and research (SISTERS) [this has not been implemented].

1967   Plowden — Children and their Primary Schools (CACE England)

The Plowden Report examined primary education in England 'in all its aspects'. Based on extensive research, it concluded that parents' attitudes to education were of supreme importance in influencing children's educational success — more so than the parents' educational or occupational status, than material circumstances at home, and than schools themselves. It approved of 'progressive', child-centred teaching methods, a broader curriculum and increased parental involvement; it recommended that schools should become more involved in their communities — suggesting that there should be positive discrimination to help schools in deprived or 'educational priority areas' (EPAs). It also recommended expansion of nursery provision, the ending of corporal punishment in primary schools, and greater attention to the needs of slow learners, handicapped children and the children of immigrants. It argued that more teachers should be encouraged into primary schools (especially men, graduates and those who had specialised in maths or science), and a new group of staff called 'teachers' aides' should be recruited with a similar status to nursery assistants [never widely implemented]. It suggested that primary education could be reorganised into first and middle schools. [The Plowden Report had a profound effect on the way both professionals and parents viewed primary education, but few of its practical recommendations were immediately acted upon. Teachers in 'difficult' schools received an extra £75 annually (as against £120 recommended by Plowden). An expansion of nursery provision did not begin until 1973 (and was cut back not long afterwards). Money was found for school building projects, especially in

EPAs, but ten years later 20% of all primary pupils were still being educated in pre-1903 buildings, many with outside lavatories. A programme of action research was set up to establish and monitor EPAs. The concept of greater parental involvement was favourably received, and this involvement has increased in the years since Plowden. Corporal punishment was forbidden in *all* state schools from 1987.]

1967   Gittins — Primary Education in Wales (CACE Wales)

Set up at the same time as Plowden, with the same terms of reference and some overlap of membership, this report shared Plowden's philosophy of education, and reached similar general conclusions. (See 1967 Plowden.) In addition, it considered some specifically Welsh issues, mainly the prevalence of two languages in school and community, but also the existence of large rural areas with sparse population, and the high respect widely felt for education and for teachers. It recommended a considerable increase in the advisory staff employed by LEAs, and in in-service training for teachers; improved co-ordination of primary education in Wales; and the fostering of both Welsh and English, especially Welsh as a second language in predominantly English-speaking areas.

1968   Newsom — Public Schools Commission, First Report

This commission was set up by a Labour government to advise on the future of boarding public schools in the light of comprehensivisation. It concluded that they could be abolished, integrated into the maintained system, or allowed to remain but without their traditional tax privileges — though the commission's terms of reference favoured integration. Public schools were defined as those belonging to the Headmasters' Conference, Governing Bodies Association or Governing Bodies of Girls' Schools Association. The commission recommended, as a step towards integration, that a number of public schools should accept some of their pupils (eventually at least half) from maintained schools, using criteria of comprehensive selection and social needs (rather than selection according to ability); these pupils would receive financial assistance. These arrangements should be voluntary if possible, but statutory if necessary. [The recommendations met considerable opposition and were never implemented.]

1968   Summerfield — Psychologists in the Education Service

It was recommended in this report that the educational psychologist's brief should be extended beyond the traditional testing and assessing of children plus some remedial teaching to include 'an extended range of treatment'. (Treatment had previously been the responsibility of the psychiatrist within the Child Guidance Service.) It also recommended an increase in the numbers of educational psychologists, aiming at a ratio of one per 10,000 children.

1968   Dainton — The Flow of Candidates in Science and Technology into Higher Education

The swing away from science in the sixth forms of secondary schools, which ran counter to the expansion of science and technology in the universities, was the subject of this investigation. The report called for changes in the sixth form, less specialisation and some mathematics for all pupils. [The recommendations were not well received, and came up against a shortage of appropriately qualified teachers and the determination on the part of the grammar and public schools to defend the Crowther notion of sixth form study in depth.]

1969   Haslegrave — Technician Courses and Examinations

The committee reviewed the training of technicians and recommended the establishment of a Technician Education Council and a Business Education Council, to oversee courses and examinations. [These were set up, and later amalgamated to form the Business and Technician Education Council (BTEC).]

1970   Donnison — Public Schools Commission, Second Report

The terms of reference for this commission were similar to Newsom's in 1968, but concerned with independent day schools and direct grant schools. The report recommended that they should either admit pupils without charging fees and without selecting by ability, or forgo state aid. [Direct grant schools were required to choose either comprehensivisation or withdrawal of state aid in 1975.]

1972   James — Teacher Education and Training

The James Report examined the arrangements for the education, training and probation of teachers in England and Wales, looking at course content, the role of different types of institution, and the relationship between intending teachers and other students. It proposed a radical reorganisation of teacher training to involve three stages (referred to as 'cycles'): general higher education, professional training and in-service training. The first cycle could take the form of a degree or a new qualification, a two-year Diploma in Higher Education. The second cycle would consist of a year's professional studies followed by a year as a 'licensed' teacher (replacing the existing probationary year), after which students would be awarded a BA (Ed). The third cycle, of in-service training, should amount to at least a term's worth every seven years for all teachers in post. [There was strong opposition to the 'licensed teacher' proposal from the teachers' unions, and little action was taken to try to implement this. The principle of integrating teacher training into higher education was accepted by the government, and throughout the 1970s colleges of education merged with other FE establishments, such as technical and art colleges, to form colleges and institutes of higher education.]

1973 Russell — Adult Education: A Plan for Development

After examining non-vocational adult education in England and Wales, this report suggested little change in the existing division of responsibility for adult education between LEAs, the university extra-mural departments and voluntary bodies such as the WEA. However, it did recommend the establishment of a national development council, regional advisory councils, and local organisations in every LEA, with a strengthening of the role of central government in both financial support and guidance to LEAs. It advised that employees should have a right to paid educational leave, and also that adult education courses should charge fees, but that these should be small. [No action on the report was taken until 1977, when the Advisory Council for Adult and Continuing Education was set up: a central body like the proposed national development council but lacking the strong government support called for by the report. The local organisations have not been established.]

1974 Finer — One-Parent Families

This report examined the particular needs and problems of one-parent families (one in ten of families with children by 1971), and many of its recommendations had educational implications: expansion of day care and nursery provision, encouragement of pregnant schoolgirls to continue their education, radical changes in the secondary school curriculum and in the careers guidance offered to girls to enable them to compete equally for better paid, traditionally male jobs, greater home–school contacts with more support from guidance staff for children known to be in one-parent families. [The Finer Report was not debated in parliament until over a year after it was published, and few of its recommendations on housing, law and benefits were implemented. The Sex Discrimination Act of 1975 provided the legal basis for equal opportunities for girls, but the 'radical changes' in girls' curriculum choices have not yet been introduced. Nursery and day care provision have expanded but still do not meet the demand. Care for school-age children outside school hours and in the holidays has received little attention. Little information is available on the extent to which schools are aware of, and providing for, the special needs of children from one-parent families.]

1974 Swann — The Flow into Employment of Scientists, Engineers and Technologists

A parallel report to Dainton (see 1968 Dainton), Swann investigated the flow of science and engineering graduates out of, rather than into, higher education. It concluded that the best graduates in these subjects tended to stay on at university rather than go into industry or teaching. It recommended that, in postgraduate training, there should be more emphasis on the links between the academic world and industry, and that scientists should be encouraged, in various ways, to contribute to the work of schools.

1975   Bullock — A Language for Life

'All aspects of teaching the use of English, including reading, writing and speech' was the subject of this report. It was concerned mainly with England, though it took some evidence from other English-speaking countries (including Scotland). It emphasised that it was not concerned with reading alone, arguing that reading is not a discrete skill that can be considered in isolation from general language development. The evidence on standards of reading was examined: while the committee judged these inadequate for present-day society, they found no strong evidence of actual *decline*. The report provided a lengthy and thorough account of the acquisition and use of the entire range of language skills, stage by stage, from infancy to adulthood, and the problems and difficulties that can occur. Language teaching in 2000 schools was surveyed: there was widespread commitment to basic skills, and much emphasis on formal practice. Insisting that there was no simple way in which reading and the use of English could be improved, and that improvement required 'a thorough understanding of the many complexities, and . . . action on a broad front', the committee offered 333 conclusions and recommendations; only with reluctance was it prepared to select 17 of these as its principal findings. These included exhortations addressed to teachers, schools, LEAs and public attitudes, as well as direct recommendations to the government for specific action. The committee called for greater emphasis on language at all educational levels, with increased spending on staffing, accommodation and other resources. Detailed recommendations included: that every school should have a policy for 'language across the curriculum' and a suitably qualified teacher to support it, and that LEAs should appoint special advisers to support the schools; that there should be screening procedures to identify language difficulties at an early stage, and specialist assistance available at both school and LEA level for those in need; that language in education should form part of initial training for every teacher; that in-service education in reading and language should be expanded; and that a system of monitoring be set up, using new instruments to assess a wider range of attainments than in the past and establishing new criteria for literacy.

1975   Alexander — Adult Education: The Challenge of Change

After investigating voluntary, non-vocational adult education in Scotland, the committee recommended that adult education should be combined with the youth and community service into a community education service. [Most Scottish education authorities adopted this arrangement.]

1976 Cowan — Reorganisation of Secondary Education in Northern Ireland

Ways of changing the Northern Ireland bipartite selective system (of grammar and secondary intermediate schools) to a non-selective system were investigated. The adoption of a dual system of 11–16 and 11–18 comprehensive schools was recommended; the former could have a two-form entry, but the latter required a six-form entry. Pupils could transfer from 11–16 to 11–18 schools for sixth-form courses. [These proposals were widely opposed, and they were abandoned by the new Conservative government in 1979, although much groundwork had been done in the meantime on the legal and administrative aspects of implementing them (see 1979 Benn, 1979 Dickson).]

1977 Taylor — A New Partnership for Our Schools

The arrangements for the 'management and government' of maintained schools in England and Wales were examined. It was recommended that every school have its own governing body, consisting of equal numbers of representatives of the LEA, school staff (including the headteacher *ex officio*), parents ('with, where appropriate, pupils') and the local community. The report suggested that all the powers relevant to school government should be formally vested in the LEA, but that it should delegate these as far as possible to the governing body of each school, who should in turn allow as much discretion as possible to the head. Specifically, governors should be given responsibility for defining the broad aims of the school; they in turn should invite the head and staff to devise means of pursuing them, and should themselves monitor the school's progress towards them. LEAs should provide initial and in-service training courses for governors, and all governors should attend them. [The main recommendations were implemented in the 1980 Education Act, and further extended in the 1986 Education Act; but the 1988 Education Reform Act introduced radical changes in the relationships between parents, governors, teachers, LEAs and central government (see Chapter 4).]

1977 Munn — The Structure of the Curriculum

Munn and Dunning are usually, and reasonably, considered together (see also 1977 Dunning). They were set up in close succession by the Secretary of State for Scotland to study the curriculum (Munn) and assessment (Dunning) in the third and fourth years of Scottish secondary schools; they kept in close touch with each other throughout their deliberations; and they presented their reports with complementary recommendations at the same time. The Munn Committee identified a number of problems with, and criticisms of, the traditional Scottish secondary curriculum, notably those arising from two major recent developments, the rapid expansion of comprehensive schools, and the raising of the school leaving age to 16. These had left too many pupils of average ability or below either struggling with work beyond their abilities or following 'improvised' courses. For pupils of high ability, too much of the curriculum was often taken up with preparation for exams, and too little done to stretch them in the earlier years. At the same time, new subjects were being urged for inclusion in the school curriculum. The committee recommended that the curriculum in these two years should consist of a *core* and an *elective* area. The core would consist of seven subjects, four (English, maths, PE and RE) to be taken by all pupils, the other three (a social studies subject, a science, and a creative arts subject) to be chosen from a short list. The elective area would be wide-ranging, and a further two or three options would be chosen from it. Each course should have three syllabuses of different (but overlapping) levels of difficulty to cater for pupils of different ability, with some limited opportunities for transfer between them. The first year of secondary schooling, at 12 plus in Scotland, ought not to differentiate pupils, the committee thought, but differentiation should begin in the second year, and be well established by the third. [Unlike that of England and Wales, Scotland's 'national curriculum' has not been established by law, and how much influence Munn has actually had on schools is uncertain.] (See also Chapter 10, Figure 10.3.)

1977   Dunning — Assessment for All

The Dunning Report on assessment should be taken together with the Munn Report on curriculum (see 1977 Munn). Dunning considered the assessment of third- and fourth-year pupils of all levels of academic ability in Scottish secondary schools. The committee recommended that O grades, taken only by the abler pupils, be replaced by an examination that matched comprehensive education, and that all pupils should be assessed for a single national certificate in each subject. To cater for pupils of different ability, however, and to ensure that everyone could gain a certificate, Dunning endorsed Munn's proposal for three syllabuses of different levels of difficulty, and recommended that certificates should be awarded at three corresponding levels, covering the entire ability range. These were termed Credit (the highest), General and Foundation, the last of these to be divided into Pass and CC (Course Completed). Awards should be based on continuous assessment of course work as well as on a final external examination. [The major recommendations of the Dunning Committee were accepted, and embodied in the Standard grade examination system, which has replaced O grades in Scotland (see Chapter 9).]

1978   Oakes — The Management of Higher Education in the Maintained Sector

This report identified the principal tasks for management as gathering information on supply and demand, planning for change, allocating resources and general supervision. It proposed a new division of responsibility for finance between central and local government, and a structure of regional and national bodies to advise both the Secretary of State and

LEAs on management tasks, while leaving considerable freedom of decision with both the LEAs and individual institutions.

1978   Waddell — School Examinations

This report stemmed from the recommendation of the Schools Council in the early 1970s that the dual examination systems of GCE and CSE should be replaced by a single system at 16 plus. The committee agreed that a single system was desirable, and suggested ways in which it could be implemented without excessive financial or administrative difficulty. They recommended using three modes, as in CSE, and a single grading system, though with special papers in some subjects for pupils of low or high ability. There should be regional grouping of GCE and CSE exam boards (four in England, one in Wales). They suggested that the unified courses could be offered from 1983, with the first exams in 1985. [In the event, the first GCSE courses were introduced in 1986, and the first exams took place in 1988. (See Chapter 9.)]

1978   Warnock — Special Educational Needs

The Warnock Report reviewed educational provision in Great Britain for children and young people 'handicapped by disabilities of body or mind'. It introduced the concept of 'special educational needs', recommending that it replace categorisation of children by the ten existing statutory categories of handicap. It suggested that up to 20% of the school population might have such needs at some time in their school career (previously around 2% of children had been legally classed as 'handicapped'). It also recommended that children whose needs could not be met within the resources of the ordinary school should have a record (which came to be called a 'statement') of their special educational needs drawn up by a multi-professional team. A detailed procedure was proposed for assessing and 'statementing' children with special educational needs, with parents having rights to be involved and make known their views. Wherever possible, children with special needs should be educated in ordinary schools alongside their peers (the principle of integration). [The Warnock Report strongly influenced the 1981 Education Act; see Chapter 4. See also Chapters 5 and 11 for further information about the education of children with special needs.]

1979   Keohane — Proposals for a Certificate of Extended Education (Cmnd. 7755)

The purpose of this study was: to examine proposals (from the Schools Council) for a certificate of extended education (CEE) — a single-subject qualification at 17 plus, for pupils staying on after the compulsory leaving age but not taking A levels; to study pilot schemes already in operation; and to advise the Secretary of State as to whether the CEE should be given official recognition. The report recommended approval and development on a national basis, but with modifications so as to ensure that those taking the courses were prepared for employment. The committee felt that basic communication and numeracy skills were most important for this purpose, and so it was suggested that all CEE certificates should record proficiency scores in English and mathematics. In addition, it suggested that more courses should be developed that related directly to the world of work, and had titles informative to employers. The committee did not endorse the Schools Council's wish to see CEE courses closely linked to CSE courses and grades; it would prefer to see CEE course more closely linked to FE courses (themselves in need of a simpler structure) and more vocational in emphasis.

1979   Mansell — A Basis for Choice

This was a report of a DES study group set up to consider full-time courses (mainly one-year courses) for young people of average ability and attainment, who had left school and needed neither GCE studies nor preparation for specific jobs. The group found that many such courses existed, but that they lacked co-ordination. It therefore recommended a unifying and rationalising curriculum structure, in the form of a set of criteria that existing and future courses might satisfy, with national validation but allowing scope for flexibility and local initiative. It was suggested that courses should consist of three main elements. First, there should be a common core of general education, occupying 50–60% of the course. The remainder should be tailored more to the vocational interests of the students, and be divided equally between vocational studies related to a general idea of employment and studies specific to a particular job. Students' final assessment should take the form of a profile, recording course work and subjective evaluations of abilities as well as the results of objective tests. A nationally recognised qualification should be awarded on successful completion of a validated course. The study group emphasised three principles underlying their recommendations: though not requiring an initial vocational commitment from students, courses must encourage the development of 'a realistic vocational focus' as they progress; attainment in vocational studies should receive equal recognition with academic attainment, and should not restrict future prospects; and the experience of learning is important in itself, as well as the attainment of certain levels of performance.

1979   Astin — Report of the Working Party on the Management of Schools in Northern Ireland

Set up after publication of the Taylor Report for England and Wales (see 1977 Taylor), this working party recommended that each school in Northern Ireland too (with the possible exception of small primary schools) should have a board of governors.

1979   Benn — Report of the Working Party on Voluntary Schools

This report investigated ways of allowing voluntary schools in Northern Ireland to continue (as direct grant schools) in the new non-selective system of secondary education recommended in the Cowan Report (see 1976 Cowan). [It became inapplicable when, after a change of government in 1979, the Cowan recommendations were abandoned.]

1979   Dickson — Report on Preparatory and Boarding Departments; Report on the Staffing of Secondary Schools; Report on In-service Training

These were reports of investigations of various legal and administrative aspects of the new non-selective system of secondary education recommended in the Cowan Report (see 1976 Cowan). [They became inapplicable when, after a change of government in 1979, the Cowan recommendations were abandoned.]

1980   Chilver — The Future Structure of Teacher Education in Northern Ireland

An interim report of the Higher Education Review Group for Northern Ireland (see also 1982 Chilver), Chilver investigated implications for the teacher education system of falling school rolls. It recommended that the three Belfast teacher training colleges come together on a single site. [The proposal aroused strong opposition from both Catholic and Protestant churches, and was not adopted.]

1981   Rampton — West Indian Children in Our Schools (Cmnd. 8273)

The 'Rampton Committee' was set up in 1979, late in the life of the Labour government (its membership was finalised by the new Conservative government) to investigate the education of children from all ethnic minority groups. First, though, it was required to produce an interim report on West Indian children. Research commissioned by the committee appeared to show considerable underachievement by West Indian children, on average, compared with white and Asian children. Various possible explanations were considered, with particular attention paid to racism, a factor frequently mentioned in evidence to the committee. While believing that few teachers were intentionally racist, and while not accepting that racism was the sole cause of West Indian underachievement, the committee concluded that unintentional racism (in the sense of stereotyped, negative or patronising views of West Indian children) was widespread and did influence children's performance. Other contributory causes that were suggested included the inadequacy of pre-school provision and its particular unsuitability for West Indian families; prejudice on the part of some teachers against West Indian children's use of English; inappropriate curricula and teaching materials; and the discouraging effect of the relatively poor employment prospects of West Indian school leavers resulting from discrimination in the labour market. At the same time, the committee believed, some West Indian parents did not do enough to support schools and teachers. In a long list of detailed recommendations, the committee urged institutions and organisations at all levels to recognise these problems and work to solve them. The main requirement, as they saw it, was for a change in attitude in the community at large towards acceptance of ethnic minorities. In specifically educational matters, stress was laid on both initial and in-service training of teachers to attune them to the needs of ethnic minority groups and to improve their understanding of a multicultural approach to education. (See also 1985 Swann.)

1982   Chilver — The Future of Higher Education in Northern Ireland

This was the final report of the Higher Education Review Group for Northern Ireland (see also 1980 Chilver). It set out to predict likely demand for higher education until the end of the century, and to provide guidelines for meeting it. Recommendations were that the New University of Ulster move towards more emphasis on mature students, distance learning and non-degree work; that Ulster Polytechnic increase emphasis on vocational studies; and that Queen's University Belfast continue largely as before, though with more emphasis on broadly based and part-time courses, and, where possible, three-year degree courses (instead of four-year).

1982   Cockcroft — Mathematics Counts

The subject of this investigation was mathematics teaching in primary and secondary schools in England and Wales, in the light of the mathematical needs of pupils when they proceed to further or higher education, employment and adult life generally. It attempted to identify these needs, and addressed detailed recommendations for meeting them to central government, LEAs, examination boards, teachers, training institutions and funding bodies for research and curriculum development. More general recommendations were addressed to the public at large. These included: that the diversity of pupils' abilities should be recognised, and a 'differentiated curriculum' and range of examination papers provided; that the quality of the maths teaching force be improved — by the recruitment and retention of more well-qualified mathematicians through financial incentives, flexible salary structures and guarantees of employment, and through increases in in-service training and support; that the subject should be approached by teachers in a variety of different ways, including exposition, discussion, practical work and problem solving, as well as mental and oral work; and that curriculum materials be developed reflecting a 'foundation list' of mathematical topics identified by the committee.

1982   Swinnerton-Dyer — The Support of University Scientific Research

This report investigated postgraduate education, especially as supported by such bodies as the Science and Engineering Research Council and the Social Science Research Council, and its success in meeting national manpower requirements. It recommended that the councils monitor the rates of submission of theses by research students in every university, so as to be able to impose sanctions on universities whose rates were unsatisfactory. It was also recommended that the DES should encourage postgraduate conversion courses, by means of maintenance grants, and that a single national body should be set up to identify manpower requirements and commission courses to meet them.

1982   Thompson — Experience and Participation

This was a review of the Youth Service, set up by the recently elected Conservative government. It recommended that a government minister be appointed to co-ordinate the work of all departments concerned with youth affairs, and that there should be more funding and clearer national objectives. It suggested that the Youth Service should be attempting to meet the 'crucial social needs' of the 11–20 age group, especially the unemployed, the handicapped, girls and young women, and ethnic minorities. [Most of the report's recommendations were rejected in the government's formal response two years later.]

1985   Swann — Education for All (Cmnd. 9453)

Just before what had been the Rampton Committee published its interim report (see 1981 Rampton), Mr Antony Rampton was replaced as chairman by Lord Swann. The final report — almost eight times as long as the interim — was able to cover the same ground in more detail and also to extend the coverage to a wide range of ethnic minority groups. Further research studies confirmed the earlier picture of West Indian pupils' underachievement, on average, compared with Asian and white pupils, but showed that the gap appeared to be diminishing significantly as time passed. The committee remained convinced that largely unintentional racism was an important factor behind West Indian underachievement, a claim not undermined by the high achievement of Asians, since stereotyped views of them were generally much less negative, and racism might have different effects on different groups. Of other possible causes of these disparities in achievement, IQ differences were considered at length, but not found to be a significant factor. Differences in socioeconomic conditions, however, were found to provide a partial explanation for the relatively low attainment not only of West Indian but probably also of Bangladeshi children. Socioeconomic differences themselves often resulted from racial discrimination, especially in employment and housing. The committee also considered, rather more briefly, the educational needs of Chinese, Cypriot, Italian, Ukranian and Vietnamese children, and the particular needs of Travellers' children and 'Liverpool Blacks'. The committee's general conclusion was that the response to these issues must lie in the education of *all* children, not just of ethnic minority children. All LEAs and schools must lead pupils to understand what is involved in Britain's being a multiracial and multicultural society; this must permeate all the work of schools. Racism must be fought, and inherited myths and stereotypes attacked. More detailed recommendations included giving first priority in language teaching to English. Although linguistic diversity was considered a positive asset, bilingualism in maintained schools was not supported. Separate schools for ethnic groups, though permissible in law, were not supported either. The committee believed that if its proposals were adopted, the demand for such schools would be greatly reduced. In this connection, central government and LEAs were urged to be sensitive to the wishes of some groups to have their daughters educated in single-sex schools. It suggested that more attention should be given to multicultural matters in both initial training and in-service training of teachers, and the effectiveness of racism awareness training should be investigated. It further recommended that greater effort should be made to employ and promote teachers from ethnic minority groups, though without positive discrimination or lowering of standards.

1985   Lindop — Academic Validation in Public Sector Higher Education

This report recommended a variety of methods of validation. It suggested that some polytechnics and colleges should be given complete autonomy by the Secretary of State to validate their own courses; others should be allowed more limited autonomy, in specific areas; while in yet others external validation should remain. It also proposed that there should be a national organisation to co-ordinate the activities of universities in validating public sector colleges' degree courses.

1988   Kingman — Report of the Committee of Inquiry into the Teaching of English Language

The committee was established to recommend a model of how the English language (whether spoken or written) works, which would form a basis for teacher training and professional discussion of English teaching; to recommend how and how far this model should be made explicit to pupils; and to recommend what pupils should be taught and be expected to understand by the ages of 7, 11 and 16. The model recommended is in four parts. The first describes the *forms* of English, spoken and written, at various levels from individual letters or sounds to connected discourse. These include vowel and consonant sounds, intonation and stress; the alphabet, spelling and punctuation; the formation of plurals and comparatives, and the use of metaphors and idiomatic expressions; the structure of phrases and sentences, the characteristics of verbs (such as tense, aspect, mood and number agreement), nouns, adjectives, adverbs, adjuncts, disjuncts and conjuncts; and the structure of units of discourse larger than the sentence. The second part describes *communication* by speakers or writers and *comprehension* by listeners or readers. This includes consideration of the context and type of discourse, of the intentions and attitudes of both speaker and listener, and of various processes of inference used in deriving meaning from sounds, forms and contexts. The third part describes the ways in which children *acquire* the forms of language, and *develop* their ability to use and understand them, with consideration of what might be found easy or difficult at different stages of development. The fourth part describes *variation* in English, over time and from place to place. Other dialects and creole languages differ systematically from Standard English; their forms and phrases are not 'bad grammar'. The report recommends that children should learn to write clearly and accurately in Standard English, and argues that they can be helped in this by learning to use descriptive technical terms to talk about language. But it does not favour a return to 'old-fashioned formal teaching of grammar' or learning by rote. How explicit the report's own model of language should be made to *pupils*, and when, is a matter for the professional judgement of teachers. The report favours the setting of attainment targets for children at 7, 11 and 16 (though with some publicly expressed reservations by Sir John Kingman himself about whether English can be 'mastered rung by rung' as in climbing a ladder (Nash, 1988)), and spells out in some detail what these should be. At all three stages, these targets include both skills in *using* English, and explicit knowledge *about* the language — its rules and conventions, its historical and geographical variation, and so on. Considerable attention is paid to the linguistic knowledge and skills required of teachers, and the ways in which these can best be learnt. Detailed recommendations are made about the amount and kind of training in English language teaching appropriate for primary teachers, and for English teachers and teachers of other subjects in secondary schools; the report's own model is recommended as a basis for these. As well as occupying a more important place in initial teacher training, English language should become one of the 'national priority areas' for in-service training of teachers. [The Secretary of State's immediate response to the report was to set up a new working party on English in the national curriculum, chaired by Professor Brian Cox, one of the members of the Kingman Committee.]

1988   Higginson — Advancing A Levels

The committee was set up to examine the principles that should govern GCE A level syllabuses and their assessment. It recommended a thorough revision of present arrangements. There should be more co-ordination of the work of the GCE examining boards, with more uniform standards of marking, a reduction in the number of separate syllabuses in each subject and a compulsory core common to the remaining syllabuses. A fifth of A level assessment should be based on course work rather than the final examination. The recommendation most widely noticed was that full-time students should normally study a wider range of subjects — five A levels plus one AS level, rather than three A levels as at present. [The recommendations of the report were rejected by the Secretary of State immediately on its publication.]

1989   Elton — Discipline in Schools

The committee was established to recommend action to secure the orderly atmosphere necessary in schools for teaching and learning. It judged the main discipline problem facing teachers to be not the rare serious incidents of physical aggression, but the cumulative disruptive effects of relatively trivial but persistent misbehaviour. It offered no simple diagnosis of causes, or simple remedies, but instead made a wide range of recommendations to teachers, headteachers, governing bodies, LEAs and parents. Central to these were ways of helping teachers become more effective classroom managers — in both initial and in-service training. Others include the following. Schools should attempt to create a positive atmosphere based on a sense of community and shared values. Heads' management styles should encourage a sense of collective responsibility among teachers, and of commitment to school among pupils and parents; their management training should be directed towards this. School buildings should be kept in a good state of repair and appearance. Parents need to provide their children with firm guidance and positive models of behaviour; schools should do more to prepare pupils for the responsibilities of being parents. Pupils themselves should be given more responsibility, and their non-academic achievements should be given more recognition.

Sources and further reading

Although official reports are usually best known by the name of the chairperson of the committee of inquiry that produced them, they are rarely to be found under that name in the author indexes of libraries. The official authorship of reports is varied and sometimes confusing; usually the easiest way of finding official reports in libraries is to look under the title in title indexes.

In addition to the reports themselves, the following are useful sources. Brett (1990), Chapter 28, contains summaries, mostly briefer than ours, of a wide, though still selective, range of reports, including a number not covered here; Scottish reports are particularly well represented. Corbett (1978) and Rogers (1980) have longer summaries and discussions than ours, but of a smaller number of reports.

Brett, M. (ed.) (1990) *Education Yearbook 1990*, Harlow, Longman.

Corbett, A. (1978) *Much To Do About Education*, 4th edn, London, Macmillan.

Gathorne-Hardy, J. (1977) *The Public School Phenomenon*, London, Hodder & Stoughton.

Gordon, P. and Lawton, D. (1984) *A Guide to English Educational Terms*, London, Batsford.

Mackinnon, D. (1976) *Social Class and Educational Attainment*, Milton Keynes, Open University Press (a component of OU Course E201 *Personality and Learning*).

Nash, I. (1988) Kingman sets stage for new English working party, *Times Educational Supplement*, 6 May 1988.

NICER (1984) *Register of Research 1978–82*, Belfast, Northern Ireland Council for Educational Research.

Rogers, R. (1980) *Crowther to Warnock: How Fourteen Reports Tried to Change Children's Lives*, London, Heinemann.

CHAPTER 4   LEGISLATION

This chapter summarises the main Acts of Parliament concerned with or directly relevant to education, together with a small number of particularly important ministerial circulars, regulations and orders. It is inevitably highly selective, both in the Acts it covers and in what it includes from each Act. No attempt is made to use legally precise terms or statements in the summaries. We begin with the 1870 Education Act — which in many ways represents the beginning of the modern education system — but concentrate on legislation since 1944. The 1988 Education Reform Act, seems likely to stand alongside that of 1944, if not that of 1870 itself, in the scale of its consequences for education.

Except where otherwise specified, these Acts apply to England and Wales.

1870 Elementary Education Act ('The Forster Act')

The aim of this Act was to provide elementary schools throughout the country, filling the gaps in the existing provision established by the churches, private benefactors and guilds. It divided the country into school districts, and, in those districts with inadequate provision, required school boards to be elected which would raise money through the rates to provide public elementary schools (often called 'board schools'). These schools were to be non-denominational and open to inspection. School boards were allowed to prescribe weekly fees and to pass byelaws requiring attendance by all children between 5 and 13 years of age.

1880 Education Act (The 'Mundella Act')

This Act required school boards to pass byelaws to secure attendance (although pupils older than 10 could be exempted if they had achieved a certain standard of attainment, or a satisfactory record of attendance). Fees in elementary schools were limited to 9d per week.

1888 Local Government Act

This Act created county councils and county borough councils, which were later used as the framework for educational administration (see 1902 Education Act).

1891 Education Act

In effect, made elementary education free.

1892 Education Act (Ireland)

This introduced compulsory school attendance in Ireland, and required local authorities to create School Attendance Committees to enforce it.

1899 Board of Education Act

This Act set up a Board of Education to supervise the education system.

1902 Education Act ('The Balfour Act')   *LEA*

The 1902 Act established a system of secondary education as the 1870 Act had done for elementary education, by filling the gaps in the existing provision with non-denominational state schools (they were not free until 1944). The Act abolished the school boards and replaced them with a system of local education authorities based on the county and county borough councils of the 1880 Local Government Act. In the county areas, however, responsibility for elementary education was given to non-county boroughs with a population exceeding 10,000 and urban districts with a population in excess of 20,000. These were known as Part III Authorities (and were abolished by the 1944 Act).

The new LEAs took over the responsibility to provide adequate facilities for elementary education and in addition were authorised to provide 'education other than elementary', either by setting up new secondary schools or by aiding existing ones in their area. They were allowed to raise and spend rates, within set limits, to fulfil these responsibilities. In some areas this resulted in generous secondary provision, whilst other areas did as little as possible. Section 6 of the Act stipulated that all elementary schools had to have managers and laid down how many of these should be LEA representatives. Governors for secondary schools were dealt with under regulations made under the Act between 1902 and 1908.

1906 Education (Provision of Meals) Act

LEAs were authorised by this Act to spend public money on meals for undernourished elementary school children.

1907 Education (Administrative Provisions) Act

With this Act LEAs were required, for the first time, to provide for the medical inspection of children in elementary schools.

1910 Education (Choice of Employment) Act

By enabling LEAs, if they wished, to set up Juvenile Employment Bureaux, this Act laid the foundation for a careers service.

1918 Education Act ('The Fisher Act')

The 1918 Act required LEAs to submit schemes of development, when requested by the Board of Education, to ensure that a fully national system of public education was being set up. It abolished the limits set on secondary educational expenditure in 1902, and removed the exemptions to the requirement to attend school between the ages of 5 and 14. It also abolished the 'half-time' system by which children worked for part of the day and attended school for the remainder. It recommended that school leavers aged 14 to 16 should attend 'continuation' schools for the equivalent of a day a week (this was never implemented). If they wished, LEAs were allowed to set up nursery schools or classes for children below school age, and to provide physical and social educational facilities, such as school camps. All fees for elementary schools were abolished.

1923 Education Act (Northern Ireland) ('The Londonderry Act')

This Act created County and County Borough Education Authorities, and Regional and County Borough Education Committees, in Northern Ireland. They were given powers to ensure adequate elementary and higher education within their areas; and provision was made for existing schools to transfer to these new authorities. These authorities were made responsible for the 'catechetical instruction' of children in elementary schools, according to their parents' denomination. Education was to be funded from both taxes and rates.

1930 Education Act (Northern Ireland)

The 1930 Act gave the Education Minister power to nominate up to a quarter of the membership of Education Committees in Northern Ireland (it being understood that the nominees would be clergymen); regulated the membership of School Management Committees; and required local education authorities to provide Bible instruction in any school if the parents of ten or more children demanded it.

1944 Education Act ('The Butler Act')

The Butler Act replaced almost all previous educational legislation and laid the foundation for the modern education system. It replaced the Board of Education with a Ministry of Education, and gave the Minister at the head of this a creative rather than a merely controlling function, charging him or her with promoting education in England and Wales.

- It abolished the distinction between elementary and higher education, and set up a unified system of free, compulsory schooling from the age of 5 to 15 (to be raised when practicable to 16). Pupils could receive this education in the LEAs' own schools, in schools maintained by other organisations, or, in certain circumstances (under Section 56 of the Act), 'otherwise' — in effect, at home.

- It extended the concept of education to cover the needs of those above and below school age, and to include the community's needs for culture and recreation. LEAs could provide nursery schools and classes; they could provide or finance holiday classes, camps, play schemes, swimming baths, community centres and recreation facilities; and were given the responsibility (never implemented) to ensure that all young people up to age 18, and not otherwise in education, received part-time further education by attending a 'county college' for the equivalent of one day a week.

- It created a variety of services to support the basic structure of primary and secondary education, e.g. transport, free milk, medical and dental treatment. School meals were to be provided for all children who wanted them (an obligation on LEAs removed by the 1980 Education Act).

- It formulated a relationship between the county and voluntary sectors which has lasted with little change. Voluntary schools were given the choice of becoming 'aided' or 'controlled' schools and provision was made for a few 'special agreement' schools (see Chapter 6). Standards were set to which all school premises had to conform.

- It named the Minister of Education (who became the Secretary of State for Education and Science in 1964) as the arbiter in disputes between LEAs, LEAs and governors, and LEAs and the public. He or she was given considerable powers, and had to be consulted by LEAs over their general development plans and any specific proposals to establish, close or alter schools (this changed under the 1980 Act).

- It set up two Central Advisory Councils for Education (CACE), one for England and one for Wales, to advise the Minister of Education. A number of major reports were produced in this way (see Chapter 3), but no CACE has been constituted since 1967, and later government reports have been issued by committees set up to consider particular issues.

- It laid down guidelines for religious instruction. All schools (county and voluntary) must start the day with a corporate act of worship, although parents have the right of withdrawal and LEAs may rule that it is impracticable to assemble all the pupils (e.g. in very large or split-site schools, or where pupils follow many different religions). All schools must also provide religious instruction (the only part of the curriculum prescribed by law, until the 1988 Education Reform Act), and this must be non-denominational except in voluntary schools.

- It required LEAs (in Section 34) to ascertain the needs of children in their area for special educational treatment, and recommended that they be educated in ordinary schools wherever possible. Ten categories of handicap were established, including the new 'maladjusted'.
- It required every LEA to appoint a chief education officer.
- It removed restrictions on married women teachers.

1946 Education Act

This Act specified the responsibilities of LEAs and governors for the maintenance of voluntary schools, and of LEAs in some circumstances for the enlargement of controlled schools.

1947 Education Act (Northern Ireland)

Public elementary education in Northern Ireland was abolished by this Act. In its place a unified system of primary, secondary and further education was set up. Education was to be compulsory from 5 to 15 years of age. Collective worship and religious education were to be compulsory in all county schools. Each local authority was required to estimate the needs of primary, secondary and further education in its area, and to submit plans for meeting them to the ministry. Local authorities were also required to provide books and stationery; to provide facilities for recreation and physical training; and to ascertain which children in their areas required special education, and provide special schools as necessary. The authorities were enabled to grant scholarships, and to give vocational guidance. Medical inspection was made compulsory for all children. Provision was made for the setting up of voluntary schools. Rules were laid down for the management of schools, and the provision of finance by local authorities.

1948 Employment and Training Act

The basis for a Youth Employment Service, which subsequently became the Careers Service, was established by this Act.

1948 Education (Miscellaneous Provisions) Act

This Act enabled LEAs to recover the costs of providing primary and secondary education for pupils not belonging to their area (repealed in the 1980 Education Act); and allowed LEAs to provide clothing grants.

1953 Education (Miscellaneous Provisions) Act

This Act authorised LEAs to pay for pupils to attend independent schools, and enabled LEAs to recover the costs of providing further education for students not belonging to their area (repealed in the 1980 Education Act).

1958 Education (Amendment) Act (Northern Ireland)

Local education authorities in Northern Ireland were required by this Act to set up management committees for further education institutions, with some degree of autonomy, instead of managing them directly.

1962 Education Act

The 1962 Act required LEAs in England and Wales to provide grants for all first-degree courses in accordance with national rules and income scales ('mandatory awards'), and allowed them to provide grants for further education ('discretionary awards'). It authorised the Secretary of State to award grants for postgraduate courses and for older students. (These various powers and responsibilities were modified in the 1973 and 1975 Education Acts.) It also set school leaving dates.

1963 London Government Act

Implemented in 1965, this changed the administration of education in the Greater London area by creating the Inner London Education Authority (responsible for the 12 inner London boroughs and the City) and 20 outer London boroughs, each being a separate LEA. The ILEA was unique in that it dealt only with education, whereas all other local authorities have education alongside other local government responsibilities, such as housing, transport and social services. (The 1988 Education Reform Act abolished the ILEA from April 1990.)

1964 Education Act

This Act amended the 1944 legislation which had divided schooling at age 11 between primary and secondary, by allowing the break to come between the ages of 10 and 12, to cover the development of middle schools. Such schools have to be 'deemed' either primary (normally 8–12) or secondary (normally 9–13) schools for purposes of classification.

1965 Remuneration of Teachers Act

Committees for negotiations on teachers' pay were set up by this Act, which also laid down procedures for arbitration where agreement could not be reached. (It was repealed by the 1987 Teachers' Pay and Conditions Act.)

1965 Teaching Council (Scotland) Act

This set up the General Teaching Council for Scotland to deal with the training, registration and professional conduct of Scottish teachers.

1965 Circular 10/65 Organisation of Secondary Education

This Circular declared the (Labour) government's objective of ending selection at 11 plus and eliminating separatism in secondary education. It requested LEAs to prepare and submit to the Secretary of State plans for reorganising secondary education on comprehensive lines, and offered guidance as to methods of achieving this. (This circular was withdrawn in 1970 by Circular 10/70, and effectively reinstated in 1974 by Circular 4/74 (DES)/Circular 112/74 (Welsh Office). See also the 1976 and 1979 Education Acts.)

1966 Local Government Act

This Act introduced the Rate Support Grant, made LEAs (rather than central government) responsible for paying for school meals and milk, and allocated funds (under Section 11) to local authorities for payment of staff employed specifically for the education and welfare of immigrants.

1967 Rate Support Grant (Pooling Arrangements) Regulations

Under the 1966 Local Government Act, these Regulations provided for the pooling of expenses incurred by LEAs on teacher training, advanced further education, the education of pupils not belonging to the area of any authority, and the training of educational psychologists.

1967 Education Act

Existing responsibilities of LEAs (under the direction of the Secretary of State) for controlled schools were extended to apply to middle schools.

1968 Education Acts

Two Education Acts were passed in 1968. The first allowed LEAs to establish comprehensive schools, and to convert existing schools into middle schools. The second required the establishment of boards of governors for polytechnics and other LEA-maintained colleges, and the specification of the governors' functions *vis-à-vis* those of the LEAs and of the colleges' principals.

1968 Education Amendment Act (Northern Ireland)

The 'maintained' school in Northern Ireland was created by this Act. It is a special category of voluntary school on whose management committee the education authority is represented, and for whose buildings and equipment the education authority takes financial responsibility.

1969 Children and Young Persons Act

Local authorities were given powers and responsibilities for children not receiving proper education, or in need of care and control.

1970 Education (Handicapped Children) Act

Responsibility for the education of severely subnormal children in England and Wales was transferred by this Act from the health authorities to the local education authorities; LEAs were thereafter responsible for all establishments caring for mentally handicapped children.

1970 Education (Examinations) Act (Northern Ireland)

This set up an Examinations Council, GCE Board and CSE Board in Northern Ireland.

1970 Circular 10/70 Organisation of Secondary Education

This Circular withdrew Circular 10/65, and affirmed the (Conservative) government's intention to allow individual LEAs to determine the shape of secondary education (selective or comprehensive) in their areas. (This was withdrawn, in its turn, in 1974 by Circular 4/74 (DES)/Circular 112/74 (Welsh Office). See also the 1976 and 1979 Education Acts.)

1970 Circular 18/70 (DES); 108/70 (Welsh Office) Primary and Secondary Education in Wales

The responsibility for primary and secondary education (and related school matters) in Wales was transferred from the Secretary of State for Education and Science to the Secretary of State for Wales. The Secretary of State for Education and Science retained responsibility for: further and higher education; the Youth Service; grants to community centres, village halls and adult education; the supply, training and qualifications of teachers;

and teacher misconduct cases. (Most of these, apart from teacher training, were also transferred in 1978.) HMIs remained an integrated body under the chief inspector, and would advise both Secretaries of State.

1970 Chronically Sick and Disabled Persons Act

This Act required new educational buildings to be made accessible to disabled people, unless this was incompatible with the efficient use of resources.

1971 Education (Milk) Act

The 1944 Act was amended so that free milk was provided to pupils over the age of 7 only if they attended special schools or qualified on medical grounds. (The 1980 Education Act and the 1986 Social Security Act each further restricted the supply of free milk.)

1971 Education (Amendment) Act (Northern Ireland)

This restricted the provision of free milk in Northern Ireland.

1972 Local Government Act

Implemented in 1974, this Act reduced the number of LEAs in England and Wales from 163 to 104, by creating some new and larger authorities. In the new system there were 39 counties, eight enlarged Welsh counties, 36 metropolitan districts and, as before, 20 outer London boroughs and the Inner London Education Authority (ILEA). It reaffirmed that LEAs must set up education committees and appoint a chief education officer, but the Secretary of State need no longer be consulted about the appointment of the latter.

1972 Raising of the School Leaving Age Order

The school leaving age was raised to 16 (nearly 30 years after this was recommended in the 1944 Education Act).

1973 Education Act

Postgraduate education was excluded from eligibility for LEA discretionary grants (it had been eligible under the 1962 Education Act). The Secretary of State was authorised, in some circumstances, to award supplements to LEA mandatory grants.

1973 Education (Work Experience) Act

This Act enabled LEAs to arrange for children under school leaving age to have work experience as part of their education in the last year of compulsory schooling.

1973 Employment and Training Act

This required LEAs to set up a careers service. It also set up the Manpower Services Commission (MSC) under the Department of Employment. (The MSC was disbanded as a separate organisation in 1988.)

1973 National Health Service Reorganisation Act

The school health service was transferred from LEAs to area health authorities, but LEAs were required to provide facilities for dental and medical inspection of pupils.

1974 Education (Mentally Handicapped Children) (Scotland) Act

Responsibility for the education of severely mentally handicapped children was transferred from the health authorities to the local education authorities under this Act. (It was similar to the 1970 Education (Handicapped Children) Act for England and Wales.)

1974 Circular 4/74 (DES)/Circular 112/74 (Welsh Office) Organisation of Secondary Education

This Circular withdrew Circular 10/70, and reaffirmed the (Labour) government's objectives of ending selection at 11 plus and creating a unified system of secondary education. It required those LEAs who had not already done so to submit to the Secretaries of State, by the end of the year, information about their plans for making their schools comprehensive. (See also the 1976 and 1979 Education Acts.)

1975 Education Act

The provisions of the 1962 Education Act were extended to require LEAs to award mandatory grants to students taking the DipHE, HND and initial teacher training courses, and to authorise the Secretary of State to award grants for adult education courses.

1975 Sex Discrimination Act

This Act prohibited sex discrimination in admission to schools, appointment of teachers (with exceptions for single-sex schools) and careers
advice, and stipulated that neither girls nor boys should be refused access
to 'any courses, facilities or other benefits provided' solely on the grounds
of their sex.

1975 Direct Grant Grammar Schools (Cessation of Grant) Regulations

These Regulations specified how and when direct grants were to be phased
out.

1976 Race Relations Act

This Act prohibited discrimination on the grounds of race in admission to
schools, appointment of teachers, careers advice, access to facilities and
the award of discretionary grants. 'Positive discrimination' in favour of
disadvantaged racial groups is not normally allowed, e.g. in recruitment or
promotion. In some closely defined circumstances, however, where it can
be shown that a particular racial group has a special need with regard to
education or training, access to facilities may be restricted or allocated first
to its members.

1976 Education Act

This attempted to abolish selection by ability for secondary schools. It laid
down the general principle of comprehensive education which would have
ended selection over a period (but this was repealed in the 1979 Act).
Added to the main Bill were six miscellaneous sections. One limited the
powers of LEAs to pay for places in independent schools, another
(Section 10) encouraged the education of handicapped children in ordinary
schools (but see the 1981 Education Act).

1976 Education (School Leaving Dates) Act

This Act set the date in the summer term after which children aged 16 are
no longer required to attend school.

1979 Education Act

This repealed the obligation placed on LEAs by the 1976 Education Act to
provide plans for comprehensive reorganisation.

1980 Education Act

The provisions of this Act were as follows:

- The obligation to provide free school milk and to provide school meals was removed, allowing LEAs to provide milk or meals or not as they wished, at whatever cost or standard they chose (including free milk or meals, if they wished, for families on low incomes), apart from a responsibility to provide free meals for children of families receiving Supplementary Benefit or Family Income Supplement, and to provide facilities free of charge for pupils to eat food brought from home. (These powers and responsibilities were altered in the 1986 Social Security Act.)

- The Assisted Places Scheme was created, whereby pupils can be transferred from maintained to particular independent schools, with the government paying part or all of the tuition fees; the Secretary of State was authorised to establish the details of the scheme by issuing regulations.

- It required all independent schools to be registered, and abolished the previous category of 'recognised as efficient'.

- Parents were given a right to choose the school they wanted their child to go to, although the LEA could refuse on the grounds of inefficient use of resources (and the parents could appeal).

- Parents were given rights to be represented on school governing bodies. LEAs and school governors were required to provide information to parents on such matters as criteria for admission, exam results, curriculum, discipline and organisation.

- It affirmed that provision by LEAs of education for under-fives was discretionary not compulsory.

- Section 13 of the 1944 Act, concerning the establishing, closing or altering of maintained schools by LEAs, was repealed. Now the Secretary of State's approval was required only if there were local objections to a proposal.

- It introduced greater control over the advanced further education pool (known as 'capping').

- The Secretary of State for Wales was authorised to give financial assistance to LEAs for the teaching of Welsh or the use of Welsh as a medium for teaching other subjects.

- It restricted the rights of LEAs to refuse to provide primary, secondary or further education for pupils or students not belonging to their area, and their powers to recover the costs of providing it.

1980 Education (Scotland) Act

A largely consolidating Act, this incorporated measures enacted separately during the 1960s and 1970s, and reaffirmed the legal framework for education in Scotland. It covered all types of school — public (i.e. maintained), grant-aided and independent. It empowered the Secretary of State for Scotland to issue regulations governing the conduct and the responsibilities of local education authorities. In addition, it defined the responsibilities and rights of parents; established the Scottish Examination Board to conduct Scottish Certificate of Education (SCE) examinations; set up committees for negotiating teachers' pay settlements, laying down procedures for arbitration where agreement could not be reached; and made provision for children with special educational needs.

1981 Education Act

Following the recommendations of the Warnock Report (see Chapter 3, 1978 Warnock), this Act altered the law relating to the education of children with special educational needs. It replaced the previous categories of handicap with the concept of special educational needs, defined as existing where a child has significantly greater difficulty in learning than the majority of children of the same age, or has a disability that prevents or hinders him or her from using the educational facilities normally available. LEAs were given carefully defined responsibilities, to identify the needs of children with a learning difficulty which, in the view of an LEA, calls for it to determine the provision required for the child. The Act set up a detailed assessment procedure for ascertaining these needs, giving parents the right to be consulted, and to appeal against an LEA's decision about appropriate provision. It also reaffirmed, with greater emphasis than the 1944 Act, the principle that children with special educational needs should normally be educated in ordinary schools provided that their needs can be met there, that the education of the other children does not suffer, and that it is compatible with the 'efficient use of resources'. (Parallel though slightly different laws apply in Scotland and Northern Ireland.)

1981 Education (Scotland) Act

This gave parents in Scotland the right to choose which school their child should attend.

1984 Education (Grants and Awards) Act

This allowed the government to allocate sums of money to LEAs for particular educational purposes, thus reducing the local authorities' control over how the block grant was spent. This reserved money was offered in the form of education support grants (ESGs) of up to 75% of the cost of each project, in areas of education that the Secretary of State had deemed to be important.

1986 Education Acts

Two Education Acts were passed in 1986.

The first introduced the Local Education Authorities Training Grants Scheme for in-service training of teachers (see Chapter 8).

The second Act required every maintained school to have a governing body, and set a formula for the numbers of parent, voluntary body and LEA representatives, which depended on the type and size of the school. Parent representation was strengthened. It required governors to present an annual report to parents at the school, and to arrange a meeting with them to discuss it. It gave governors the responsibility for determining sex education policy in the school, and preventing 'political indoctrination'. Governors were also to 'use their best endeavours' to ensure that children with special educational needs were identified and suitable provision made. Corporal punishment was abolished in state schools from August 1987; independent schools may still use it, but not on pupils whose fees are paid by the state.

1986 Social Security Act

From 1988, the provisions of the 1980 Education Act concerning free school meals and milk were abolished. LEAs no longer have the power to supply free school meals or milk to any children other than those from families receiving Income Support; and they no longer have any obligation to supply free meals or milk to *any* children (even those from families receiving Income Support).

1987 Teachers' Pay and Conditions Act

This Act abolished the negotiating procedures set up in the 1965 Remuneration of Teachers Act, replacing them until 1990 by authorising the Secretary of State to appoint an interim advisory committee and to impose teachers' pay and conditions. (This was extended by ministerial Order to March 1991.)

 # 1988 Local Government Act

This included an amendment (Section 28) forbidding local authorities to 'promote teaching in any maintained school of the acceptability of homosexuality as a pretended family relationship'. (There is still uncertainty as to whether this clause has any practical effect on schools, because of vagueness in the wording of the amendment. See Macnair, 1989.)

1988 Education Reform Act

The main provisions of the Act are as follows:

- It empowered the Secretary of State to prescribe a common curriculum (to be called the national curriculum) for pupils of compulsory school age in maintained schools (for details, see Chapter 10), to set attainment targets for each of its constituent subjects at the ages of 7, 11, 14 and 16, and to make arrangements for assessing how well these are met; established a National Curriculum Council (for England) and a Curriculum Council for Wales to oversee the implementation and assessment of the national curriculum; required LEAs, school governors and headteachers to ensure that the national curriculum is taught in all maintained schools. (These provisions apply to 'grant-maintained' schools (see below) They do not apply to independent schools.)

- It established mechanisms to ensure that the limits set by LEAs or governors on the number of pupils a maintained school admits are not lower than the school is physically capable of accommodating, normally the number admitted in 1979, when school rolls were at their highest. Parents may send their children to any school that has room for them, provided that it caters for their age and aptitude. (These provisions apply to 'grant-maintained' schools (see below).)

- It required LEAs to delegate certain responsibilities for financial management and the appointment and dismissal of staff to the governing bodies of schools; permitted the governing bodies to delegate many of these responsibilities to headteachers (see Chapter 8).

- It allowed a maintained secondary school, or a primary school with over 300 pupils (extended in 1990 to all primary schools), on the resolution of its governing body, with the consent of a majority of those parents who vote in a secret postal ballot, and with the approval of the Secretary of State, to opt out of LEA finance and control, and be given 'grant-maintained' status. (If fewer than half the parents vote, a second ballot must be held within 14 days. The results of the second ballot will be binding, regardless of how many parents vote in it.) The school will then own its own premises, employ its own staff, and receive an annual grant directly from central government. The character and size of a grant-maintained school cannot be altered, or the premises sold, without the consent of the Secretary of State.

- It empowered the Secretary of State to enter into long-term agreements to fund city technology colleges (see Chapter 5).

- It removed polytechnics and certain other colleges of higher education from LEA control, making them 'free-standing statutory corporations', under the direction of boards of governors whose members are initially appointed by the Secretary of State (see Chapter 5).

- It required LEAs to delegate certain responsibilities for financial management and the appointment and dismissal of staff to the governing bodies of the larger colleges remaining under LEA control.

- It placed the funding of higher education in the hands of two statutory bodies, a Universities Funding Council (UFC) (replacing the University Grants Committee), and a Polytechnics and Colleges Funding Council (PCFC) to administer funds for higher education provided directly by the Secretary of State. The councils have the power to attach terms and conditions to the provision of funds to any institution. Both bodies are to be independent of government. Their members are appointed by the Secretary of State, with between 40% and 60% of the membership to come from higher education.

- It forbade the granting of academic tenure (see Chapter 7) to new university academic staff; withdrew tenure from staff in post who move to a different university or accept promotion within the same university. At the same time it affirms that academic staff may not be dismissed for holding particular beliefs or following particular lines of inquiry, and that senior staff may not be dismissed to be replaced by more junior, and cheaper, staff.

- It abolished the Inner London Education Authority (see Chapter 6) transferring its responsibilities from April 1990 to the inner London boroughs and the City of London.

1988 Schools Board (Scotland) Act

Established school boards – governing bodies for Scottish schools, with strong parental and community representation. The boards have extensive rights to be informed and consulted about their schools' educational, disciplinary and financial policies and achievements, and to participate in the appointment of senior staff. (Their powers and duties resemble those given to English and Welsh school governors by the 1986 Education Act rather than those given by the 1988 Education Reform Act.)

1989 Self-Governing Schools etc. (Scotland) Act

Established procedures whereby Scottish schools could 'opt out' of finance and control by education authorities, and receive funding directly from the Scottish Central Government.

1989 Education Reform (Northern Ireland) Order

Northern Ireland is to follow the main thrust of the English and Welsh reforms. There will be a similar, though not identical, common curriculum and pattern of assessment, and comparable scheme for delegation of financial management to the governing bodies of schools. 'Opting out' will also be permitted, but only where a school seeks 'grant-maintained *integrated* status', and chooses to progress towards full integration of Protestant and Roman Catholic pupils.

Sources and further reading

The standard, regularly updated, reference work on educational law in England and Wales is Liell and Saunders (1989); it has a special supplement on the 1988 Education Reform Act. It is detailed and rigorous, but consequently difficult for those untrained in law to tackle. Much more approachable for the lay reader are the guides and summaries produced by the Advisory Centre for Education and the Chartered Institute of Public Finance and Accountancy. The journal *Education and the Law* is a useful source of information about new legislation, regulations, orders, DES circulars and court cases.

A number of books and booklets offer detailed summaries of the 1988 Education Reform Act as it finally passed into law. Maclure (1989) is especially valuable and up-to-date about developments after the Act itself.

Advisory Centre for Education (1988) Guide to education welfare benefits, *ACE Bulletin*, No. 22, March/April 1988.

CIPFA (1988) *Financial Information Services*, Vol. 20, *Education*, London, Chartered Institute of Public Finance and Accountancy.

Hyndman, M. (1978) *Schools and Schooling in England and Wales: A Documentary History*, London, Harper & Row.

Liell, P. and Saunders, J. B. (1989) *The Law of Education*, 9th edn, London, Butterworth.

Maclure, S. (ed.) (1986) *Educational Documents, England and Wales, 1816 to the Present Day*, 5th edn, London, Methuen.

Maclure, S. (1989) *Education Re-Formed: a guide to the Education Reform Act*, 2nd edn, London, Hodder & Stoughton.

Macnair, M. R. T. (1989) Homosexuality in schools — Section 28, Local Government Act 1988, *Education and the Law*, Vol. 1, No. 1, pp. 35–9.

Sallis, J. (1981) *ACE Guide to Education Law*, London, Advisory Centre for Education.

CHAPTER 5 INSTITUTIONS

This chapter describes, with some basic facts and figures, the range of institutions that make up the United Kingdom's education system.

FACT

The United Kingdom has some 35,000 schools in total, with just under half a million teachers and over nine million pupils (1987–8 figures: Government Statistical Service, 1989, Tables 10 and 15).

(A) Pre-school

Pre-school provision by an LEA may take the form of:

- *Nursery schools* — Separate schools for 2–5-year-olds, each with its own headteacher and a number of classes staffed by teachers and nursery assistants who have trained under the National Nursery Examination Board (NNEB). The recommended child/adult ratio is 13 to 1 (or 22 to 1 if qualified teachers only are counted).

- *Nursery classes within primary schools* — Separate classes for 3–5-year-olds which are an integral part of a primary school, with staffing as for nursery schools.

- *Reception classes* — Children who are just under compulsory school age can gain early admission to the first (reception) class in an infant or first school.

There is no obligation on LEAs to provide pre-school education (except for children identified as having special educational needs) and provision varies greatly, both in amount and in type. In Wales, 69% of 3- and 4-year-old children go to maintained nursery or primary schools, compared with 45% in Northern Ireland, 44% in England and 39% in Scotland (CSO, 1989a, Table 2.4). Considerable variation in amount and type of provision is also found between regions and between individual LEAs. (This is illustrated for England in Figures 5.3 and 5.4.)

Pre-school children may also attend *day nurseries*, which are provided by local authority Social Services Departments, and regulated by the Department of Social Security. Private provision, including *playgroups* and *childminders*, has to be registered with local authority Social Services Departments. In 1987, in the United Kingdom, some 33,000 children attended local authority day nurseries, 174,000 went to registered childminders and another 477,000 went to registered playgroups (CSO, 1989b, Table 3.8). Figure 5.1 shows how these forms of provision have changed over time.

There are also *independent schools* that cater for pre-school children.

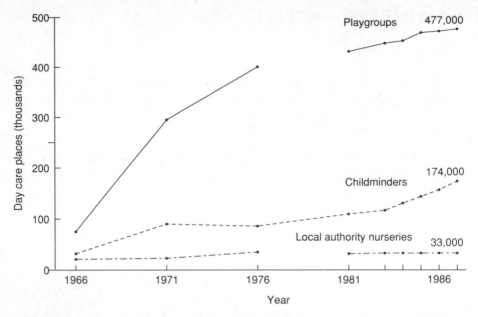

Figure 5.1   Number of pre-school places in establishments registered with Social Services Departments (i.e. forms of pre-school provision that are not part of the education system), United Kingdom 1966–87
(Adapted from CSO, 1987, Table 3.1; 1989b, Table 3.8)
Note: Playgroups include registered nurseries up to 1976; local authority nurseries include local authority playgroups up to 1976

These are two main types: those that are basically preparatory schools — preparing very young children for entry to a highly academic independent school later on — and those that are a fee-paying alternative to maintained nursery schools, either because pre-school places are in short supply or because the school adopts a particular educational philosophy, such as the Montessori method. Since 1979 they too have been required to register with local authority Social Services Departments, and are not counted in the official education statistics.

Some common patterns of early childhood experience are shown in Figure 5.5.

FACT

In the United Kingdom in 1988, there were 1298 publicly maintained nursery schools catering for some 98,000 children, 82% of them on a part-time basis. But the majority of under-fives received their education in primary schools, in either nursery or reception classes — 557,000 children in 1988, 44% of them part-time. Another 40,000 under-fives went to private schools, 58% of them part-time. Altogether just under half (48%) of the 3- and 4-year-old population received some education at school, mostly on a part-time basis (Government Statistical Service, 1989, p. iv and Table 16).

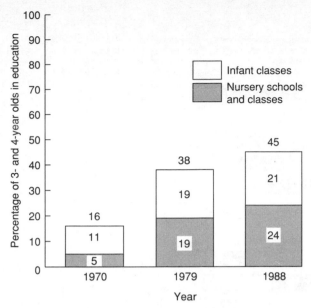

Figure 5.2   Percentage of 3- and 4-year-olds in LEA-provided education, England
1970–88
(Adapted from DES, 1989b, Table 3)

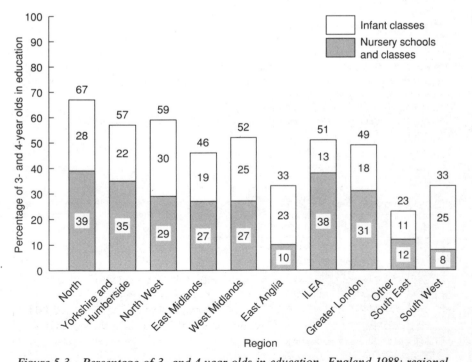

Figure 5.3   Percentage of 3- and 4-year-olds in education, England 1988: regional
variations
(Adapted from DES, 1989c, Table 1)

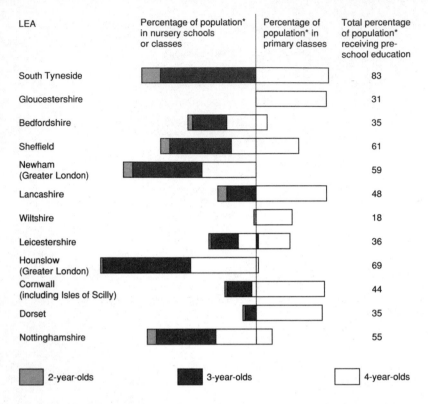

Figure 5.4 Percentage of 2-, 3- and 4-year-olds in education, England 1988: variations among selected LEAs (*Expressed as a percentage of the estimated total population of 3- and 4-year-olds)
(Adapted from DES, 1989b, Table 1)
Note: Any category with a percentage figure of less than 1 is omitted from the diagram

	0 year	1 year	2 years	3 years	4 years	5 years	6 years
Child 1	Childminder or day nursery			Nursery class		Primary class	
Child 2	Home		Nursery school			Primary class	
Child 3	Home			Nursery class		Primary class	
Child 4	Home			Playgroup		Primary class	
Child 5	Home					Primary class	
Child 6	Combined nursery centre					Primary class	
Child 7	Home			Private nursery		Preparatory school class	

Figure 5.5   Some common patterns of early childhood experience

(B) Primary

The legal definition of primary education covers children aged 5–11 years in England, Wales and Northern Ireland, and 5–12 years in Scotland. Primary schools consist mainly of:

- *Infant schools* — for children aged 5–7 years.

- *Junior schools* — for those aged 7–11 years.

- *Combined junior and infant schools* — these are the most common and cater for children of both age groups.

An alternative system, introduced in some areas in the late 1960s, is the three-tier system, of *lower* (or *first*), *middle* and *upper schools*, based on the idea that the age of 8, 9 or even 10 was a more appropriate time for children to make the transition between the informal teaching of the early years and the more formal subject teaching offered later.

Middle schools developed in a variety of patterns; some catered for 8–12-year-olds (deemed primary), others for 9–13-year-olds (deemed primary or secondary at the discretion of the LEA) and yet others for 10–14-year-olds (deemed secondary). Middle schools are confined almost entirely to England; in 1988–9 Scotland had only two middle schools and Wales one (CSO, 1989b, p. 88).

Centres for teaching English as a second language (CE2L) are separate schools that have been set up by a few LEAs. They provide basic English language tuition to children whose mother tongue is not English, before they enrol in ordinary school. There were 7 such centres in England in 1988, all catering for primary age children (DES, 1988, Table A1).

FACT

In the United Kingdom in 1988, there were nearly 25,000 maintained primary schools, including 586 middle schools deemed primary. Almost all were mixed-sex schools. Between them they taught 4.6 million children and employed 206,000 teachers (81% female). The numbers of both pupils and teachers have increased slightly since 1984 — the first increase since the early 1970s. Non-maintained schools accounted for another 252,000 or so children of primary age (Government Statistical Service, 1989, Tables 12 and 16; DES, 1988, Table A1).

Size of schools
Almost two-thirds of all primary schools have between 100 and 300 pupils. Very small schools (50 children or less) accounted, in 1987–8, for around 10% of primary schools in the United Kingdom, but the proportion varied greatly from region to region. For example, 18% of the primary schools in Wales and in Northern Ireland, and 24% in Scotland, had 50 pupils or less, compared with 8% in England as a whole, and 0.2% in Greater London (CSO, 1989a, Table 9.4).

School closures and falling rolls
Between 1980 and 1988, more than 1500 maintained primary schools
closed in the United Kingdom (see Figure 5.6).

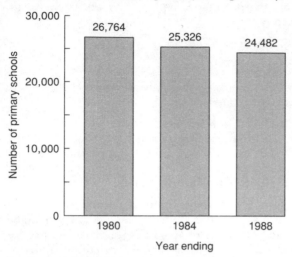

Figure 5.6   Numbers of primary schools, United Kingdom 1980–8
(Adapted from Government Statistical Service, 1983, 1985 and 1989, Table 2)

These closures have to be seen in the context of changes in the number of
children of primary school age; this is illustrated in Figure 5.7, using data
for England. After more than a decade of decline, the numbers have been
rising since 1985.

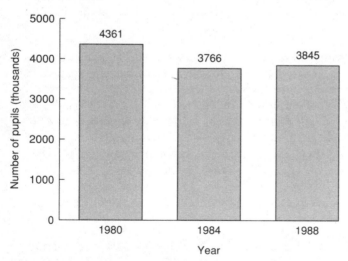

Figure 5.7   Primary school rolls, England 1980–8
(Adapted from DES, 1989c, Table 1)

Over the entire period, the number of primary school teachers also fell
(despite a slight rise since 1984). The overall effect (in England) was a

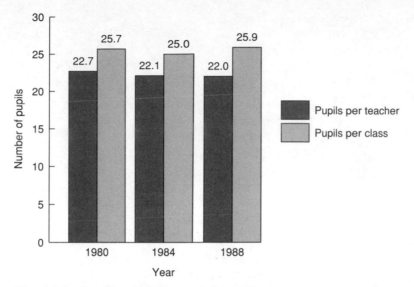

Figure 5.8   Pupil/teacher ratios and class sizes in primary schools, England 1980–8 (Adapted from DES, 1989c, Tables 3 and 4)

small reduction in the pupil/teacher ratio, but a slight increase in the average size of classes. This is illustrated in Figure 5.8.

The pupil/teacher ratio in maintained primary schools varies from country to country. Compared with the United Kingdom average of 22 to 1, it is rather higher in Northern Ireland (23.5 to 1) and lower in Scotland (20.3 to 1) (CSO, 1989a, Table 9.1: 1988 figures. See also Chapter 8, Part 2 (C)).

(C) Secondary

Secondary education is compulsory up to the age of 16, and pupils can stay on at school for up to three years longer. The following list of types of secondary schools includes some that no longer exist and others that now exist only in very small numbers, often in just a few LEAs.

Tripartite system

Grammar, secondary modern and technical schools in England and Wales (and, with different terminology, in Scotland and Northern Ireland — see below) form what is called the tripartite system, though in reality technical schools have never existed in large numbers. The tripartite system now forms a very small and highly localised part of secondary schooling in Great Britain, where maintained secondary education is now almost entirely comprehensive (see Figure 5.9). The principal characteristics of tripartite schools are as follows:

- *Grammar schools* provide a mainly academic education for pupils aged 11 to 19 who have been selected on the basis of ability.

- *Secondary modern schools* provide a general education for those who do

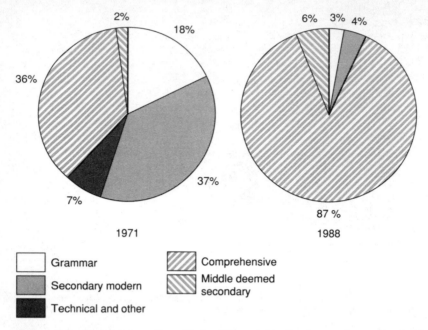

Figure 5.9 Percentages of pupils in different kinds of secondary school, United Kingdom 1971 and 1988
(Adapted from Government Statistical Service, 1989)

not go to grammar schools, usually up to the minimum school leaving age (though pupils can stay on longer).

* *Technical schools* provide a general education but with considerable emphasis on technical subjects. These never existed in large numbers and are now virtually extinct: by 1988, only one remained in England (DES, 1988, Table A1).

In Scotland, the closest equivalent to English and Welsh grammar schools were called *senior secondary schools*, while the equivalent of secondary moderns were *junior secondary schools*. (However, the phrase 'grammar school' does sometimes appear in the names of particular schools in Scotland.)

In Northern Ireland, a selective system still predominates, though with a few comprehensive schools in certain areas. The closest equivalent to English and Welsh grammar schools are called *grammar secondary schools*; they can, however, accept some fee-paying pupils. (The schools called 'grammar preparatory schools' are fee-paying primary schools attached to voluntary grammar secondary schools (see Chapter 6); very few grammar preparatory schools remain.) Corresponding to secondary moderns are *secondary intermediate schools*. Until the mid 1970s, Northern Ireland also had *technical intermediate schools*, corresponding to the English technical schools, but none exist now. About one-eighth of secondary pupils in Northern Ireland attend grammar secondary schools, the remainder attending secondary intermediate schools.

Direct-grant schools
Phased out by 1980, they used to bridge the gap between the maintained and independent sectors, being grammar schools which took fee-paying pupils but also provided free places for able children from poorer homes who were financed by a direct grant from the government. They were given the choice of becoming part of the maintained system or becoming independent; most chose the latter.

Grant-aided schools
In Scotland, these were schools that received part of their maintenance expenditure from the government. They were phased out by 1986. In Northern Ireland, 'grant-aided' is the term equivalent to 'maintained' in Britain.

Comprehensive schools
Comprehensive schools take all pupils (except those attending special schools) regardless of ability. There is a great variety of schemes and great variation in the degree to which schools are fully comprehensive: if some schools in an area take the children who are thought to have greater academic ability, the remaining schools, even if called comprehensive, cannot be considered fully so.

Secondary schools with sixth form
These cater for the full age range from 11 (or following middle schools from 12, 13 or 14) to 18 or 19 years. In 1986 there were 1945 comprehensive schools with sixth forms in England, with over 200,000 pupils.   *GCSE A level*

Secondary schools without sixth form   *O level.*
These cater only for children up to the age of 16. Those pupils wishing to continue their education have either to transfer to a school which does have a sixth form or to a sixth form college, or to move outside the secondary school system into a tertiary or further education college (see below).

Sixth form colleges
Sixth form colleges are separate schools for 16–19-year-olds. They usually take pupils from several 'feeder' comprehensives without sixth forms in the area. They may provide non-academic as well as academic courses, but academic courses predominate. In 1973 there were 21 sixth form colleges in England; by 1988 there were 104, catering for over 64,000 pupils. Their growth is partly a response to the falling numbers of secondary pupils, which has made it difficult for many smaller schools to make up viable sixth form classes in less-popular A level subjects. They generally cater for up to 500 students. As they operate under school regulations they cannot admit part-time or older students.

Community schools
These are maintained schools which provide education for school pupils and mature students alongside social, recreational and cultural activities for the whole community.

City technology colleges
These new, relatively small, selective colleges are to be set up by private
sponsors, with government grants to provide a free education with a
technological emphasis for 11–16-year-olds. The school day and terms are
likely to be longer than the legal requirement for state schools. City
technology colleges (CTCs) will be independent of LEAs: the DES will
pay running costs but promoters will own or lease the premises and be
responsible for their management, employing teachers, etc. By the end of
1989, three CTCs had opened (in Solihull, Nottingham and Teesside).

FACT

**Comprehensive schools are now (1987–8 figures) by far the most
common form of secondary education for pupils in England (86%),
Wales (98%) and Scotland (99%). But Northern Ireland retains a
largely selective system, with 88% of its secondary pupils in secondary
intermediate schools, and 12% in grammar secondary schools (Government Statistical Service, 1989, Table 18).**

Figure 5.9 shows, for the whole of the United Kingdom, how the pattern of
secondary school provision changed between 1971 and 1988, with a
decrease in the number of grammar, secondary modern and technical
schools (or their equivalents), and a corresponding increase in comprehensive and 'middle-deemed-secondary' schools.

Size of schools
Secondary schools are generally much larger than primary schools; only
9% have fewer than 300 pupils on the roll and the most common size is
between 600 and 1000 pupils (CSO, 1989a, Table 9.4).

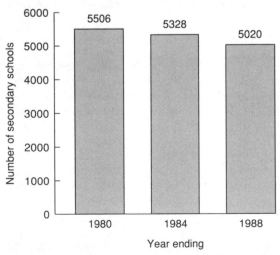

*Figure 5.10   Numbers of secondary schools, United Kingdom 1980–8
(Adapted from Government Statistical Service, 1983, 1985 and 1989, Table 2)*

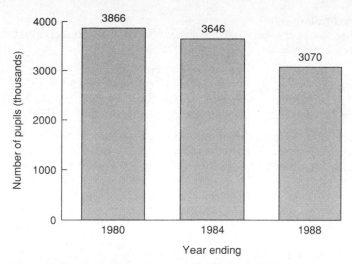

Figure 5.11   Secondary school rolls, England 1980–8
(Adapted from DES, 1989c, Table 1)

The pupil/teacher ratio in United Kingdom maintained secondary schools was 15.4 to 1 in 1988. However, there are variations from country to country. In particular, the ratio is rather lower in Northern Ireland (14.5 to 1) and especially in Scotland (13.0 to 1) (CSO, 1989a, Table 9.1. For changes in the pupil/teacher ratio, see Figure 5.12 below; see also Chapter 8, Part 2 (C)).

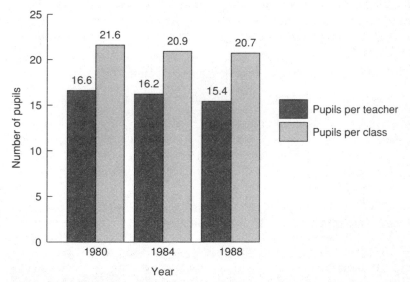

Figure 5.12   Pupil/teacher ratios and class sizes in secondary schools, England 1980–8
(Adapted from DES, 1989c, Tables 3 and 4)

School closures and falling rolls
In the United Kingdom, between 1980 and 1988, 486 maintained secondary schools closed (see Figure 5.10).

These closures have to be seen in the context of changes in the number of children of secondary school age; this is illustrated in Figure 5.11, using data for England. The numbers are declining, and are expected to continue declining until 1992, when they will begin to increase again (DES, 1989c).

During the same period, the number of secondary school teachers also fell, but not by enough to prevent a slight reduction in both the pupil/teacher ratio and the average size of classes. This is illustrated in Figure 5.12, again using data for England.

(D) Special

Special schools provide education for children with special needs, on the grounds that they cannot be educated satisfactorily in an ordinary school. They are generally much smaller than mainstream schools: 83% of special schools in the United Kingdom have 100 pupils or fewer; 99% have 200 or fewer (1987–8 figures). Special schools often take the full age range, including nursery and post-16. They have a lower pupil/teacher ratio than any other type of school: 6.3 to 1 in the United Kingdom in 1987–8 (Government Statistical Service, 1989, Tables 14 and 15).

FACT

In 1987–8 there were 1908 special schools in the United Kingdom, including 80 hospital schools and 92 assisted independent schools, attended by 118,000 pupils. About three-quarters of them were day schools and the remainder boarding (Government Statistical Service, 1989, Table 17).

Special classes and units may also be provided in mainstream schools (especially primary) for children with particular needs, e.g. the partially hearing or partially sighted, 'disruptive' children or slow learners. In England in 1986, the numbers of such units officially recognised by the DES were 1247 in primary schools and 660 in secondary schools. In addition, there are many other units not officially recognised — 'disruptive units', 'remedial classes', 'sanctuaries', etc.

The percentage of children with different types of handicap in special schools are shown in Figure 5.13 for England in 1982 — the last year for which such data were collected. Since the 1981 Education Act (see Chapter 4) came into force in 1983, children assessed as having special educational needs are given an individual 'statement' of these needs instead of being assigned to a category of handicap (see Chapter 3, 1978 Warnock). In 1988, 138,000 children in England had statements of special educational needs — 1.9% of the total school population. As Figure 5.14

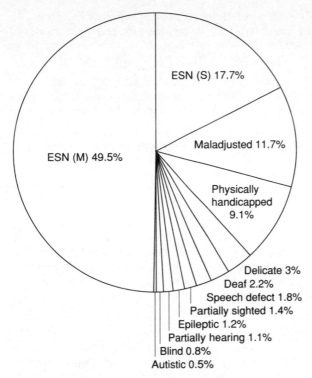

Figure 5.13   Categories of handicap of pupils, aged 5–15, attending special schools, England 1982
(Adapted from DES, 1986a)

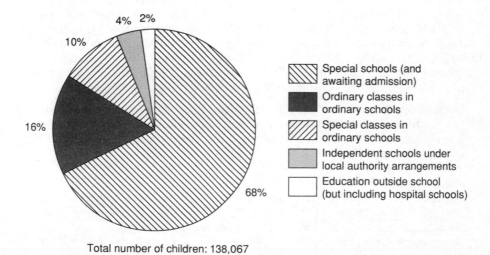

Figure 5.14   Educational provision for children with statements of special educational need, England 1988
(Adapted from DES, 1988, Table A25)

shows, the great majority (68%) of children with statements are educated in special schools, and a further 10% are in officially recognised special classes and units in mainstream schools. About 16% are educated in ordinary classes in mainstream schools (DES, 1988, Tables A3 and A25).

Since the 1981 Act, the percentage of the United Kingdom total school population educated in special schools has fallen slightly, from just under 1.4% in 1980–1 to just over 1.3% in 1987–8 (Government Statistical Service, 1989, Table 14).

See Chapter 11 for more detailed facts and figures on special education.

(E) Independent

Independent schools are those outside the maintained education system. They are not funded by the government or local authorities, and most charge fees (see Chapter 11); a few are wholly charitable institutions. All independent schools have to register with their LEA (or with the local authority Social Services Department in the case of independent nursery schools) and they can be inspected by HMIs.

The majority of independent schools provide a highly academic main-stream education for pupils selected on the basis of ability (usually through an entrance examination), but some are based on alternative philosophies of education, and others offer specialised provision: for example, for the musically gifted, for children with special needs, for children of foreign nationals, or for religious minorities. Independent schools generally have a relatively low pupil/teacher ratio — 11.5 to 1 in 1987–8, compared with 17.1 to 1 in all schools (combined figures for primary and secondary schools) (Government Statistical Service, 1989, Table 14). About a quarter of pupils at independent schools are boarders, a much higher proportion than in maintained schools. Boarding is particularly common in the well-known public schools, but is available in many of the preparatory schools from the age of 8. Public schools normally take children from the age of 13 (usually the boys' boarding schools) or from the age of 11.

Independent schools are also referred to as public schools, private schools, preparatory schools and non-maintained schools. The terms are used loosely and sometimes interchangeably, but the most common meanings appear to be as follows.

Public schools
Especially in England, this term traditionally refers to independent, fee-charging, but non-profit-making, secondary schools belonging to various highly prestigious associations. However, many of these now prefer the term 'independent schools', as in the title of the Independent Schools Information Service (ISIS). Associations about which ISIS collects and distributes information include the following. (The figures are for 1990.)

- *Headmasters' Conference (HMC)* — The most prestigious of associations of independent schools, and also the largest, including around two hundred schools, with some 153,000 pupils in total, 83% of whom are boys (many of the HMC schools admit girls only in the sixth form). Twenty-nine per cent of HMC school pupils are full or weekly boarders.

- *Society of Headmasters of Independent Schools (SHMIS)* and *Governing Bodies Association (GBA)* — The SHMIS and GBA schools are also predominantly for boys (74% of their 22,000 pupils). Forty-three per cent are full or weekly boarders.

- *Girls' Schools Association (GSA)* and *Governing Bodies of Girls' Schools Association (GBGSA)* — The GSA and GBGSA schools are almost exclusively for girls (98% of their 119,000 pupils); 19% are full or weekly boarders.

- *Independent Schools Association Incorporated (ISAI)* — The ISAI schools have some 58,000 pupils, with roughly equal numbers of boys and girls; 8% of these are full or weekly boarders.

Overall, just under 50% of pupils in these schools are boys, just over 50% girls (ISIS, 1990).

In Scotland (as in most of the rest of the world), the term 'public schools' usually refers to maintained schools. The term is not used in Northern Ireland, although a few of the voluntary schools (see Chapter 6) belong to the Headmasters' Conference.

Non-maintained schools
This is the term used in the official government statistics for the United Kingdom to include both independent schools (in Great Britain) and voluntary grammar schools (in Northern Ireland).

Private schools
'Private schools' has a narrow sense, now slightly archaic, in which it refers to schools run for profit by teacher–entrepreneurs (a minority, especially at secondary level); in this sense, the term 'private schools' is *opposed* to 'public schools', which are not profit-making. However, the phrase 'private school' is nowadays more often applied to non-maintained schools generally; in this sense, it *includes* public schools.

Preparatory schools
These schools take children between the ages of about 8 and 13 and prepare them for competitive entry to the public schools. Many belong to the Incorporated Association of Preparatory Schools (IAPS), which has approximately 114,000 pupils, of whom 71% are boys. Twenty per cent of pupils in IAPS schools are full or weekly boarders (ISIS, 1990).

FACT

In 1987–8 there were 2548 non-maintained (assisted and independent) schools in the United Kingdom, excluding the non-maintained special schools. They provided education for some 621,000 children, 6.8% of the total school population (less in Wales and Scotland but more in Northern Ireland, where voluntary grammar schools are included) (Government Statistical Service, 1989, Tables 2 and 14).

Children may move between the independent and maintained sectors at different stages of their school career; many different patterns of schooling are possible, some of these are illustrated in Figure 5.15.

See Chapter 11 for more facts and figures on independent schools.

Age

	5	8	11	13	16	18
Pupil 1	State primary school		Independent secondary school		Sixth form in local comprehensive	
Pupil 2	Preparatory school		Independent secondary school for girls		Co-ed sixth form of boys' public school	
Pupil 3	State first School	Preparatory school (boarding)		Independent public school	State sixth form college	
Pupil 4	State primary school		Independent co-educational secondary school			

Figure 5.15   Some patterns of schooling

(F) Tertiary

The third stage of education covers all non-compulsory, post-school education. The term 'further education' (FE) is used sometimes in a general sense to cover all post-school education, but in practice it is usually differentiated from higher education (study at universities, polytechnics and colleges of higher education), and divided into the categories of *non-advanced further education* (NAFE), which means A-level standard or below, and *advanced further education* (AFE) which is above A level or its equivalent. Degree courses at polytechnics and colleges of higher education are sometimes referred to as advanced FE. More often, though, they — like degree courses at universities — are termed *higher education*.

There is a wide range of institutions offering further education in the United Kingdom. Until the 1988 Education Reform Act most in England were funded by and under the control of LEAs. Now the larger ones are independent of LEAs and are funded by the Polytechnics and Colleges Funding Council (PCFC). Smaller colleges remain under LEA control.

Tertiary colleges
Tertiary colleges combine the functions of a sixth form college and a further education college. They are open to students of all abilities, and provide a wide range of vocational and academic courses. Some cater for several thousand students, full- and part-time. There were 41 tertiary colleges in England in 1987 (DES, 1988a, Table F9).

Colleges of further education

There are more than 400 colleges of further education in England alone, about 60% of them classified as large (over 1000 full-time-equivalent students). They offer a mixture of advanced and non-advanced FE, and go by a variety of titles, including colleges of further education, colleges of agriculture and horticulture, technical colleges, colleges of art and colleges of commerce (DES, 1988a, Table F9).

Colleges and institutes of higher education

These resulted, in the 1970s, from the integration (in England and Wales) of teacher training outside universities with the rest of further education. Many of the original colleges of education merged with other FE establishments such as technical and art colleges to form colleges and institutes of higher education (around 55 in England by the mid 1980s). As well as teaching qualifications, they generally provide other degree and diploma courses, and so are similar to polytechnics and universities, although usually much smaller in size. Scotland still (1987–8) has five colleges of education and Northern Ireland two.

Voluntary colleges

There were 23 voluntary colleges of higher education in England and Wales in 1985, catering for the equivalent of approximately 25,000 full-time students. Most of the colleges were originally established by religious foundations to train teachers for schools, but they now offer a wide variety of other courses, mainly at degree level. They receive grants from the government and the majority are overseen by the National Advisory Board for Local Authority Higher Education.

Polytechnics

Polytechnics came into existence after 1966, often resulting from the merging of two or more FE colleges. Until 1988, they were under the control of LEAs; now they are 'free-standing statutory corporations' under the direction of boards of governors, half of whose membership consists of people experienced in industry, business, commerce and the professions; the other half consists of representatives of staff, students and LEAs, together with co-opted members. In 1987–8 there were 29 polytechnics in England and one in Wales, catering for a quarter of a million students; of these, 95% were on advanced courses. Courses at polytechnics are often multi-disciplinary, made up from a variety of individual 'modules', and often have a vocational or technical emphasis. Polytechnics frequently have close links with business and industry, and unlike university students, many polytechnic students have jobs and study on a sandwich (20% of students) or part-time (25% of students) basis (DES, 1988a, Table F9).

Polytechnics offer degree courses (validated by the CNAA), including higher degrees, plus other types of advanced further education, such as the BTEC Higher National Certificates and Diplomas. They also offer some non-advanced courses, although the majority of these are taken at other FE colleges.

The student population at polytechnics is growing much faster than that of universities. Between 1979 and 1987, the number of full-time students taking higher education courses at polytechnics and colleges increased by 40% (and that of part-time students by 38%) (DES, 1989a, Table 1).

Northern Ireland now has no polytechnics; in 1985 its one polytechnic merged with the former New University of Ulster to become the University of Ulster. (For Scotland, see *Central Institutions*.)

For basic statistics of student numbers, see Figures 5.16–5.18 below.

Central Institutions
Scotland has 16 Central Institutions, which are similar in function to polytechnics in England and Wales, though they have always been controlled centrally by the Scottish Education Department rather than by local education authorities.

Independent further education colleges
A number of FE colleges outside the publicly maintained system offer full- and part-time courses in subjects such as art and architecture, drama, languages, and English for foreign students. Their qualifications are validated either by the British Accreditation Council for Independent Further and Higher Education (BACIFHE) or by one of the independent professional bodies such as the National Council for Drama Training or the Council for Dance Education, or are the college's own non-validated certificates or diplomas. Tutorial colleges, sometimes known as 'crammers', are privately run establishments offering intensive courses to prepare students for particular examinations, usually O or A levels.

Universities
There are 49 universities in the United Kingdom. Of these, six are 'ancient' (Oxford, Cambridge, St Andrew's, Glasgow, Aberdeen and Edinburgh), and 31 are 'new' (established since 1945 — often on the basis of an existing institution of higher education). Normally their undergraduate courses occupy three or four years of full-time study — though this does not apply to the Open University (OU), whose students are part-time, or to the independent University of Buckingham, whose first-degree courses last two years.

The Department of Education and Science has responsibility for universities in Scotland and Wales as well as England (responsibility was transferred from the Treasury in 1964). Northern Ireland's universities are the responsibility of the Department of Education Northern Ireland. But universities have a considerable and jealously guarded degree of independence. They operate under Royal Charters, appoint their own staff, decide on their own admissions policies and have traditionally had academic freedom in their teaching and research, though the last of these has arguably been eroded in recent years by the 'earmarking' of government funds for specific subjects, and the need to seek sponsors for particular projects.

With two exceptions, all universities receive central government funding that is allocated among them on the basis of advice by the Universities Funding Council (UFC) rather than by the direct decision of the DES. The exceptions are the University of Buckingham, which receives no government funds, though its students are eligible for mandatory grants, and the OU, whose funds are allocated directly by the DES.

In 1987, British universities (other than the OU) had some 246,000 undergraduate students and 55,000 postgraduate students. Just over 90% of university students are full-time (DES, 1989b, Tables 1 and 4). The student population of universities is growing, though less steadily and much more slowly than that of polytechnics. Between 1979 and 1987, the number of full-time university students rose by 4%. The number of part-time university students on degree courses (other than OU students) rose in the same period by 36% (DES, 1989a, Table 1).

The Open University, established in 1969, teaches by correspondence and broadcasting, and has no entrance qualifications for its undergraduate courses: admission is on a 'first come, first served' principle. It has by far the largest number of students of any university in the United Kingdom, with approximately 72,000 undergraduate students in 1990, almost all studying part-time, plus over 3000 postgraduate students and an estimated 200,000 students taking short continuing education courses. It accounts for two-thirds of all part-time undergraduate students in British universities (OU Public Relations Dept, 1990; DES, 1989a).

The largest conventional university is the University of London (in effect a federation of largely independent colleges), which has over 40,000 students, followed a long way behind by the Universities of Wales, Oxford, Cambridge, Leeds and Manchester, each of which have over 10,000 students.

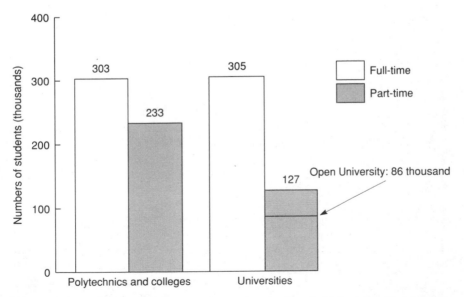

Figure 5.16 Numbers of full-time and part-time students in higher education by type of institution, Great Britain 1987 (Adapted from DES, 1989a, Table 1)

Just under half of all university students (excluding OU students) live in colleges, halls of residence, or other accommodation provided by their university; another third live in lodgings or privately rented accommodation; and the rest live at home.

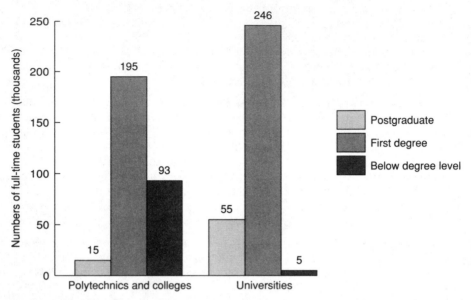

Figure 5.17   Numbers of higher education students taking full-time courses of different levels by type of institution, Great Britain 1987
(Adapted from DES, 1989a, Table 4)

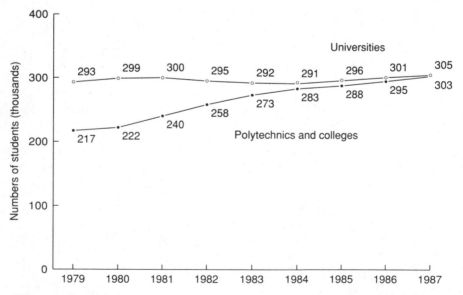

Figure 5.18   Numbers of full-time higher education students by type of institution, Great Britain 1979–87
(Adapted from DES, 1989a, Table 1)

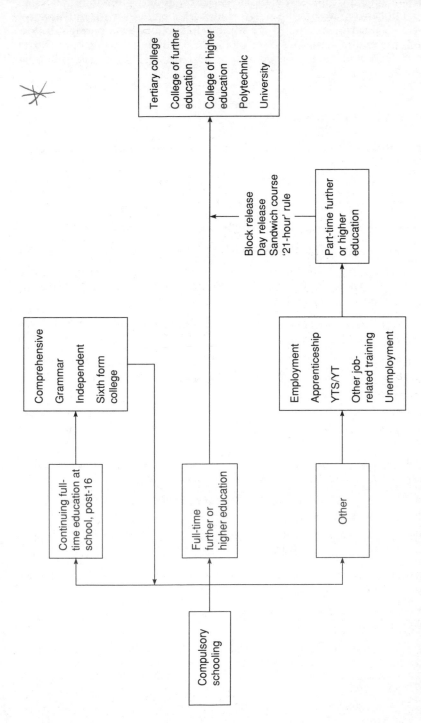

Figure 5.19 Further education and training

Figures 5.16–5.18 give some basic statistics about student numbers in higher education, comparing polytechnics and colleges with universities. Figure 5.19 illustrates some of the routes that school leavers might follow through the main institutions offering further and higher education. (More detailed facts and figures on education and training after school can be found in Chapter 12.)

Sources and further reading

Central Office of Information (1990) *Britain 1990: an official handbook*, London, HMSO.

CSO (1987) *Social Trends*, No. 17, 1987 edition, London, HMSO.

CSO (1989a) *Regional Trends*, No. 24, 1989 edition, London, HMSO.

CSO(1989b) *Social Trends*, No. 19, 1989 edition, London, HMSO.

DES (1985) *The Education System of England and Wales*, London, HMSO.

DES (1988a) *Statistics of Education: Further Education 1987*, London, Department of Education and Science.

DES (1988b) *Statistics of Education: Schools 1988*, London, Department of Education and Science.

DES (1989a) *Statistical Bulletin 4/89: Student numbers in higher education — Great Britain 1975 to 1987*, London, Department of Education and Science.

DES (1989b) *Statistical Bulletin 7/89: Pupils under five years in each local education authority in England*, London, Department of Education and Science.

DES (1989c) *Statistical Bulletin 8/89: Statistics of Schools in England — January 1988*, London, Department of Education and Science.

Government Statistical Service (1983) *Educational Statistics for the United Kingdom 1983*, London, HMSO.

Government Statistical Service (1985) *Educational Statistics for the United Kingdom 1985*, London, HMSO.

Government Statistical Service (1989) *Educational Statistics for the United Kingdom 1989*, London, HMSO.

ISIS (1990) *Annual Census 1990*, London, Independent Schools Information Service.

OU Public Relations Dept (1990) *Fact Sheet Number 1: an introduction to the university*, Milton Keynes, The Open University.

CHAPTER 6 ORGANISATION AND CONTROL

Education in the United Kingdom is administered as a partnership between local authorities and central government, though the balance of power and influence between the partners is at present changing in England and Wales, with local authorities losing powers. The exact division of responsibilities between central and local authorities varies from country to country, though in most respects England and Wales are more similar than the other countries. At central level, there are four government departments, one in each country, and at local level, each country is divided up into administrative areas for educational administration. Local education authorities in England, Wales and Scotland are subsidiaries of the wider local councils, but those in Northern Ireland are not so closely linked to the rest of local government.

England and Wales

The central government department responsible for education in England is the *Department of Education and Science* (DES). Its responsibilities cover all schools (maintained and independent), and further and higher education in England, including universities, although in practice much of the latter is delegated to the *Universities Funding Council* (UFC) and the *Polytechnics and Colleges Funding Council* (PCFC). The DES is also responsible for universities in Wales and Scotland.

The DES has a staff of around 2500. At its head is a cabinet minister, the Secretary of State for Education and Science. He or she is supported by a Minister of State and two Parliamentary Under-Secretaries of State. These are the posts that change with a change of government. The civil servants who staff the DES remain in post irrespective of changes of government. At their head is the permanent secretary, supported by three deputy secretaries (with responsibility, respectively, for schools, further and higher education, and teachers) plus a legal adviser (heading the legal branch) and the senior chief inspector (head of Her Majesty's Inspectors, or HMIs, who are attached to the DES but independent of it).

Figures 6.1–6.3 show the main branches, and within them the divisions, under the control of each of the three deputy secretaries. They illustrate how the DES is concerned with all aspects of education, though at a broad, policy-making level; the administration of most of the areas is at present the responsibility of the LEAs. In addition to the branches under the control of these three deputy secretaries, there are also a legal branch, a finance branch, an organisation branch (dealing with staffing and accommodation within the DES) and a library.

The *Welsh Office Education Department* is responsible (and has been since 1970) for schools and further and higher education in Wales, but not universities or the qualifications, probation, pay, superannuation or misconduct of teachers, which remain the responsibility of the DES.

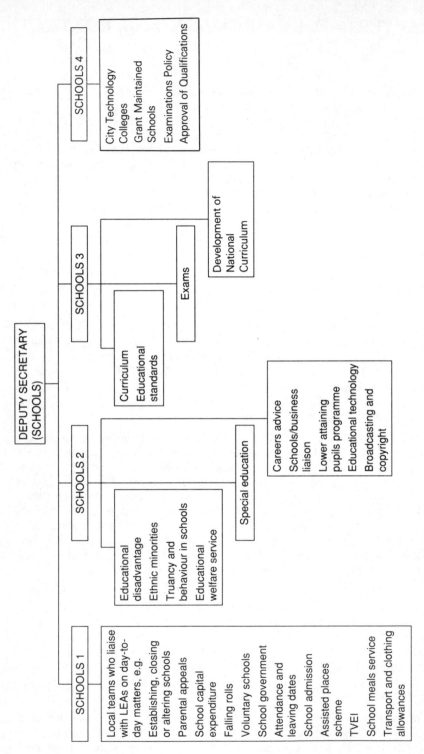

Figure 6.1   Branches of the DES: (i) Schools

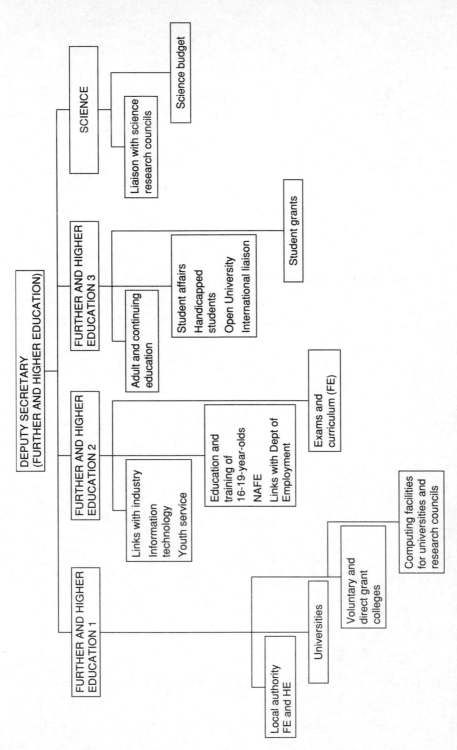

Figure 6.2   Branches of the DES: (ii) Further and higher education

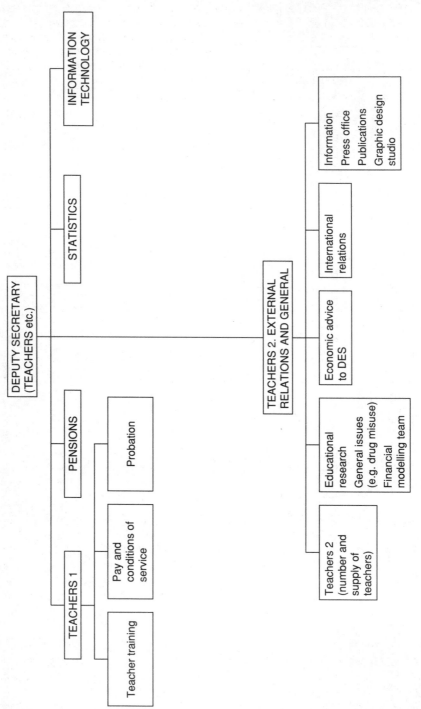

Figure 6.3   Branches of the DES: (iii) Teachers etc.

England has 109 *local education authorities* (LEAs) — corresponding to 39 counties (plus the Scilly Isles), 36 metropolitan districts, 20 outer London boroughs and 12 inner London boroughs plus the City of London. Wales has eight LEAs, each corresponding to a county. The current boundaries of English and Welsh LEAs date from 1974, apart from those of inner London. The inner London boroughs (and the City of London) became local education authorities only in April 1990, on the abolition of the Inner London Education Authority (ILEA). (See Figures 6.4–6.6.)

The LEAs in England and Wales are subsidiaries of the wider local councils and function through *education committees*. Elected councillors form the majority on these committees and have ultimate authority and responsibility for them, although in practice the education officers, who remain in post while councillors come and go, are often very influential. In most LEAs the education committee is composed of various sub-committees: usually one for finance, at least one for schools (in larger authorities there may well be separate ones for primary, secondary and special schools), at least one for further education (which may be sub-divided into youth and community work, adult education and recreation), and one each for careers, libraries and museums, and sites and buildings.

Central versus local control
The 1944 Education Act set up a national educational system which was locally administered. Central government, in the form of the DES, had overall responsibility and made policy decisions, but LEAs had control over most of the day-to-day running of the system. In the 1980s the balance of power shifted increasingly away from the LEAs and towards central government on the one hand, and individual schools and colleges on the other. This was reflected in:

- The introduction of *education support grants*, whereby central government sets aside money for educational topics it deems to be of particular importance. LEAs have to bid for these grants.

- The replacement of the Schools Council (abolished 1981) with two centrally appointed committees: the *Schools Curriculum Development Committee* (SCDC) and the *Secondary Examinations Council* (SEC).

- The increased involvement of government departments other than the DES in education. These include: the *Department of Employment*, which (directly and indirectly) runs YTS/YT and TVEI (see Chapter 10) and controls 25% of the funding for NAFE (see Chapter 5); the *Department of the Environment*, which through the Urban Programme gives grants for educational projects in deprived areas; and the *Department of Industry*, which through the Micros in Schools Project subsidises the buying of microcomputers in primary and secondary schools.

The LEAs' power was further diminished by the 1988 Education Reform Act, in two major ways. First, the Act required LEAs to delegate important responsibilities to the governing bodies of all but the smallest schools and colleges, in particular the responsibility for managing a school's budget and setting its own spending priorities, and for appointing (and dismissing) members of staff. An LEA is not allowed to use the

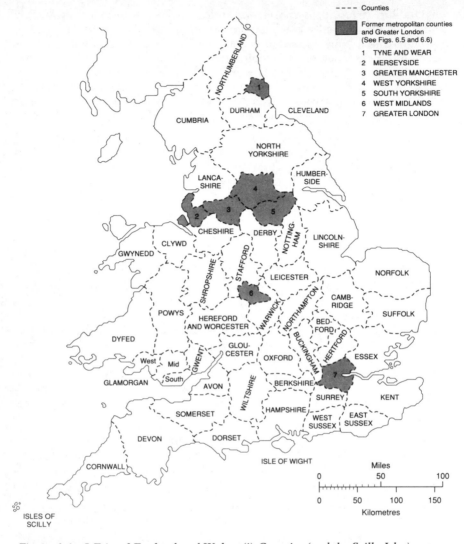

--- Counties

[dark square] Former metropolitan counties
and Greater London
(See Figs. 6.5 and 6.6)

1 TYNE AND WEAR
2 MERSEYSIDE
3 GREATER MANCHESTER
4 WEST YORKSHIRE
5 SOUTH YORKSHIRE
6 WEST MIDLANDS
7 GREATER LONDON

*Figure 6.4   LEAs of England and Wales: (i) Counties (and the Scilly Isles)
(Adapted from OPCS, 1987)*

allocation of funds to schools as a means of enforcing its policies. Funding
levels must be determined by a standard formula, drawn up by the LEA
but approved by the Secretary of State. It must place most weight on the
numbers of pupils in the school, and must be applied even-handedly across
all the authority's schools. This scheme has become known as the *Local
Management of Schools* (LMS) (see Chapter 8). Secondly, the Act laid
down procedures whereby individual schools could opt out of local
authority control, acquiring *grant maintained status*, and receiving their

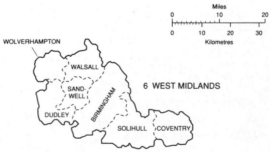

Figure 6.5   LEAs of England and Wales: (ii) Metropolitan districts (Adapted from OPCS, 1987)

funding directly from the DES (see Chapter 4: 1988 Education Reform Act). By summer 1990, 44 schools had successfully applied for grant maintained status. The extent to which control has moved out of the hands of the local authorities can be seen in Figure 6.7, where an asterisk (*) indicates a power traditionally held by the LEA which can now be taken over by schools which 'opt out'; a dagger (†) indicates new powers which central government has taken on since 1979, often transferred from the

INNER LONDON (formerly ILEA)

1   CITY OF LONDON
2   ISLINGTON
3   CAMDEN
4   WESTMINSTER
5   KENSINGTON AND CHELSEA
6   HAMMERSMITH AND FULHAM
7   WANDSWORTH
8   LAMBETH
9   SOUTHWARK
10 LEWISHAM
11 GREENWICH
12 TOWER HAMLETS
13 HACKNEY

Figure 6.6   LEAs of England and Wales: (iii) London boroughs (and the City) (Adapted from OPCS, 1987)

LEA; and a double dagger (‡) in the parents or governors column indicates new duties and rights they have received since 1979.

The control of schools

The 1944 Education Act created a unified framework which brought the church schools under state control (turning them into maintained schools), but left them with varying degrees of independence, usually over religious matters, according to how much financial support the church continued to provide. This system has remained relatively unchanged (apart from a recent increase of the proportion of parent and teacher representatives on the governing bodies of voluntary schools).

DES	LEA	Headteacher	Parents	Governors
Policy making	Provide 'adequate and efficient' education at primary and secondary level (nursery optional)	Care of pupils ('in loco parentis')	Send child to school (or 'educate otherwise')	Oversee implementation of national curriculum, conduct and discipline‡
Inspecting all schools and institutions (except universities) to ensure standards	Establish, alter and close schools (after giving public notice)	Internal organisation of school	Express preference for a school‡	Financial management of school‡
Supply and training of teachers	Finance schools* and local education service	Rules, discipline, curriculum (subject to national curriculum and governors' general direction)	Be represented on governing body	Appointment and dismissal of teachers‡
Final court of appeal in disputes between parents and LEA	Enforce school attendance		Receive published information about school‡	Suspension/expulsion of pupils
Management of public sector higher education† (via NAB)	Student grants (England and Wales)		Be involved in assessment procedure for children with special educational needs‡	Sex education‡
Providing education support grants†	Identify and provide for special educational needs		Withdraw child from religious instruction	Use 'best endeavours' to identify children with special educational needs‡
Assisted places scheme†	Health and safety		Decide whether a school should 'opt out' of LEA control‡	Publish information for parents about the school‡
Financing universities (via UFC) and polytechnics and larger colleges (via PCFC)†	Careers service			
Collecting statistics	Ensure equal opportunities for both sexes and all races			
Educational building programme				

Figure 6.7 Powers and duties

The LEAs created by the 1944 Act could set up new schools themselves; these are called *county schools*. Schools that had been established by a church body (or occasionally a trust) became *voluntary schools*, of which there are three types: 'aided', 'controlled' and 'special agreement', differing mainly in the extent to which the LEA finances and controls them.

- *Aided schools* (4368 in number in January 1988, roughly half Church of England and half Roman Catholic) provide their own premises and meet some of the maintenance costs in exchange for a degree of control.

- *Controlled schools* (3116 in number, virtually all Church of England) provide their own premises, but the LEA meets all the schools' costs. Before the 1988 Act, the governing bodies had control only over religious instruction.

- *Special agreement schools* are few in number (84, most of them Roman Catholic), and they arose from the government's offer in 1936 to pay 50–75% of the cost of building new secondary schools. By the outbreak of the Second World War, very few of the 500 or so 'special agreements' made with voluntary bodies had been implemented, and the 1944 Act allowed for their revival.

The main differences in funding and control between the different types of school are summarised in Figure 6.8.

Voluntary schools in England account for about a third of primary schools and a fifth of secondary schools (see Figure 6.9). The majority of voluntary primary schools are Church of England, while just over half of voluntary secondary schools are Roman Catholic (see Figure 6.10).

Scotland

The central government department responsible for education in Scotland is the *Scottish Education Department* (SED). Its responsibilities are for schools and further and higher education (excluding universities, which are the responsibility of the DES, but including central institutions and teacher training). At local level, there are nine regional and three islands area education authorities (EAs). The current boundaries date from 1975 (see Figure 6.11).

The control of schools
Scotland does not have voluntary schools. Church schools which have chosen to transfer to the education authority, rather than be independent, become public schools (the term used in Scotland for maintained or state schools), although they can make separate arrangements for denominational instruction. Most are Roman Catholic, but there are also (in 1986) one Jewish, one Episcopalian and one Sikh school.

Northern Ireland

The central government department responsible for education in Northern Ireland, the *Department of Education Northern Ireland* (DENI), has

	Maintained schools				Independent schools
	County	Voluntary			
		Aided	Controlled	Special agreement	
Established by:	LEA	Voluntary organisations, usually church bodies — C of E, Church in Wales, Roman Catholic Church, Jewish organisations		Voluntary organisations usually church bodies — but by special agreement the LEA paid $\frac{1}{2}$ to $\frac{3}{4}$ cost of building a new school	Private individuals Benefactors Trusts and charities
Financed by:	LEA	Voluntary body responsible for external repairs and maintenance (assisted by 85% LEA grant) LEA pays running costs, internal repairs and teachers' salaries	LEA	Voluntary body responsible for external repairs and maintenance (assisted by 85% LEA grant)	Parental fees Assisted places scheme Benefactors/charities
Controlled by:	LEA and governing body Must offer non-denominational religious instruction to all pupils	Voluntary body appoints $\frac{2}{3}$ majority of governors, and hence controls admissions and appointment of teachers Can offer denominational instruction to all pupils	LEA appoints majority of governors, but voluntary body nominates a third Can offer denominational instruction to families who request it	Voluntary body appoints majority of governors	Board of Governors (DES can enforce minimum standards for premises and staffing)

Figure 6.8   The administration and control of schools in England and Wales

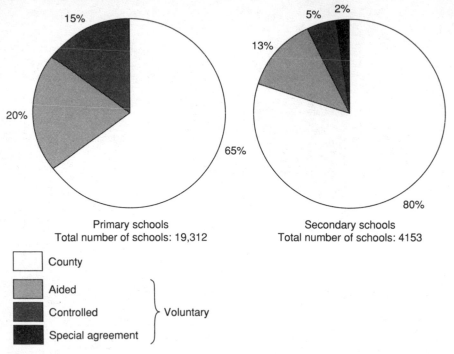

Primary schools
Total number of schools: 19,312

Secondary schools
Total number of schools: 4153

County

Aided ⎫
Controlled ⎬ Voluntary
Special agreement ⎭

*Figure 6.9   Type of control of maintained schools, England 1988
(Adapted from DES, 1988, Table A13)*

overall responsibility for schools, further education and universities. Local
education authorities in Northern Ireland are called *Education and Library
Boards*, and are responsible for the local provision and administration of
schools and further education, as well as university awards. There are five
of these; their current boundaries date from 1973 (see Figure 6.12). Unlike
the local education authorities in Great Britain, Education and Library
Boards in Northern Ireland are appointed centrally, by the head of the
DENI, though their membership includes nominated representatives of
district councils, as well as teachers, local community representatives,
trade union nominees, churches and maintained school trustees (see
below).

The control of schools

Northern Ireland uses the terms 'controlled', 'voluntary' and 'maintained',
but with different meanings from those that apply in England and Wales.
There are three principal types of school management, described below; in
all of them, the representation of parents and teachers has been strengthened, and that of the churches reduced, since 1984.

- *Controlled schools* are managed by education and library boards
  through boards of governors. The schools may be primary, secondary
  intermediate, grammar or special; membership of boards of governors
  differs for the different types of school, but they include representatives

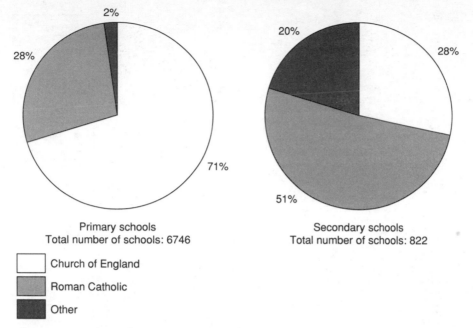

Figure 6.10   Denominations of voluntary schools, England 1988
(Adapted from DES, 1988, Table A13)
Note: 'Other' includes 16 primary and five secondary Jewish schools, and 28 primary
Methodist schools (DES, 1988, Table A12)

of parents, teachers, education and library boards, and sometimes churches (mainly the Protestant churches). The capital expenditure and running costs of controlled schools are met by the Education and Library Boards from funds provided by the DENI. (A *controlled integrated school* is a possible type of school under the 1978 Education (Northern Ireland) Act. The aim was to facilitate the development of schools which would be attended by pupils of different faiths. The proposal to change to a controlled integrated school has to be supported by three-quarters of the parents. No such schools as yet exist.)

- *Voluntary (maintained) schools* are managed by boards of governors, which consist of representatives of trustees (mainly Roman Catholic), parents, teachers and Education and Library Boards. Capital expenditure on these schools is partly met (up to 85%) by the DENI; running costs are met by the Education and Library Boards. There are several integrated primary voluntary (maintained) schools, and one integrated post-primary (Lagan College).

- *Voluntary (non-maintained) schools* are managed by boards of governors, whose constitution varies from school to school, but which include representatives of parents and teachers, and sometimes of the DENI or an Education and Library Board. They are mainly grammar schools; there are separate Protestant and Roman Catholic schools.

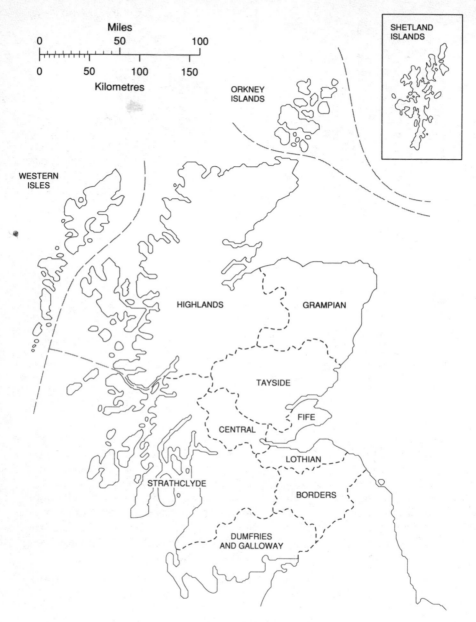

Figure 6.11   Education authorities in Scotland
(Adapted from OPCS, 1987)

Capital expenditure on these schools is partly met (up to 85%) by the DENI; running costs are met from block grants direct from the DENI and from fees (although for many pupils these are paid or assisted by the Education and Library Boards).

*Figure 6.12   Education and Library Boards in Northern Ireland
(Adapted from OPCS, 1987)*

Sources and further reading

DES (1986) *The DES — A Brief Guide*, London, HMSO.

DES (1988) *Statistics of Education: Schools 1988*, London, Department of
Education and Science.

Wallis, E. (1986) *Education A–Z: Where to Look Things Up*, London,
Advisory Centre for Education.

CHAPTER 7   THE PROFESSIONALS

(A) Introduction

The education service employs a wide variety of staff. Apart from those whose job is to teach (in schools, further education colleges, polytechnics and universities), there are the administrators, advisers and inspectors; the support staff who assist teachers (e.g. nursery assistants and laboratory assistants); the ancillary workers who maintain premises, provide the meals service and run the offices; and the professionals who offer specialist services, such as the educational psychologists.

FACT

Out of a total workforce of 1,847,000 in 1989, local authorities in England and Wales employed 944,000 (51%) in the education service; 537,000 of these (29% of all employees) were teachers and lecturers. These figures represent a reduction in staffing levels since 1979 — of 4% for all employees, 6% for those in education (CIPFA, 1989).

Figure 7.1 groups jobs in education into five main categories, although in practice the boundaries (e.g. between administrators and advisers) are not always well defined, and the term 'ancillary staff' is sometimes used to cover jobs categorised as 'educational support' too. All of the staff in Figure 7.1 are employed by the LEA, apart from those in universities, polytechnics and larger colleges; and the HMIs, who are employed by the DES. However, the 1988 Local Government Act requires that a local authority's cleaning and maintenance work be put out to competitive tender: this is likely to result in fewer of these staff being employed directly by the LEA in future. And as the 1988 Education Reform Act takes effect, teachers, though still formally employed by LEAs, will be appointed, and may be dismissed, by the governors of their schools.

(B) The staff of the education service

This section gives a brief description of the principal posts in the education service, at the level of central government, LEAs and schools. This is followed by some more detailed facts and figures about the teaching profession, and a description of some of the professionals involved in further and higher education.

Central government level

Her Majesty's Inspector (HMI)   The HMIs are an independent group who, in England, are attached to the DES. Their main job is to report to the Secretary of State on the education provided in schools and colleges (since

LEA administrators	Teaching staff (schools)	Education support staff	Other education professionals	Ancillary staff	Further and higher education
Director of education/chief education officer (CEO)	Headteacher	Welfare assistant	Educational psychologist (EP)	Administration and clerical	Vice chancellor/Principal/Director
Deputy CEO	Deputy head	Nursery assistant	Education welfare officer (EWO)	Kitchen and canteen	Professor
Assistant education officer (AEO)	Second master/mistress	Teacher's aide	Adviser	Caretakers	Principle Lecturer
Professional assistant	Senior teacher	Student assistant	Youth and community worker	Porters	Reader
	Teacher	Laboratory technician	Careers officer	Gardeners	Senior lecturer
	Nursery teacher	Media resources officer	Schools-industry liaison officer	Cleaners	Lecturer
	Special school teacher	Librarian	Her Majesty's Inspector (HMI)	Security staff	Research fellow
	Peripatetic teacher	Medical staff			Research officer
	Supply teacher				Research associate
	Home liaison teacher				Research assistant
	Home tutor				
	Educational home visitor				

Figure 7.1   Jobs in the education service
(Adapted from CIPFA, no single date)

1983, all formal HMI reports have been published), and to give professional advice to the DES. They are also involved in in-service teacher training and disseminating central government thinking on curriculum and practice. HMIs are allowed to inspect any school, private as well as maintained, and all colleges of further and higher education maintained by LEAs or receiving money from public funds, but not universities (except by invitation). In 1985 there were around 500 HMIs in England and Wales. Most of them are locally based and each is responsible for a group of schools or colleges; they are under seven divisional inspectors. There are also about 65 staff inspectors based at the DES who have national responsibilities for particular areas of the curriculum or aspects of education, such as maths teaching or special educational needs.

At the head of Her Majesty's Inspectorate is the senior chief inspector, with seven chief inspectors under him or her, each of whom is responsible for co-ordinating the work of staff and divisional inspectors in several areas of education (one chief inspector is responsible for pre-school and primary education, educational disadvantage and multiracial education, for example; and another for the curriculum 5–16, local advisory services, LEA inspections and independent schools).

Scotland, Wales and Northern Ireland have their own HMIs, whose chief inspectors report to their respective education departments.

Local education authority level
As local management of schools takes effect, many of the LEA posts described below are likely to change in character and probably lose some current functions.

Chief education officer (CEO)   Every LEA is required to have a chief education officer (known in some authorities as the director of education), who is the senior appointed official, with overall administrative responsibility for the running of the local education system. He or she is accountable to the education committee, on which elected councillors form the majority (see Chapter 6). There are 117 chief education officers in England and Wales.

Deputy chief education officer   He or she co-ordinates the assistant education officers (see below), and deals with major initiatives such as secondary school reorganisation.

Assistant education officer   An assistant education officer is in charge of one of the half dozen or so branches into which the work of the education service is divided, such as secondary education or further education.

Professional assistant   This is a first-level administrative post within an education department, usually for an experienced teacher. He or she works under an assistant education officer. The post is sometimes also known as administrative assistant.

Adviser (sometimes called inspector)   Advisers are employed by the LEA to advise on the content and quality of courses, organise in-service training of teachers and, in some authorities, to inspect schools and colleges. They are usually responsible for a particular field, such as computing, pre-school provision, adult education, political education or equal opportunities. There is no uniformity of numbers; some large authorities have 50 or more advisers while a few LEAs have none, relying on the centrally appointed HMIs for inspection and advice. In 1981–2 there were 1850 LEA advisers employed in England and Wales.

Educational psychologist Every LEA has a team of educational psychologists headed by a principal educational psychologist. They generally have a psychology degree, a teaching qualification, some teaching experience and further specialist training. They work with children who have behavioural and/or learning problems in school, administering tests (traditional IQ testing used to be a central part of the job, but it is becoming less important) and designing remedial work in conjunction with teachers. Some educational psychologists visit the schools in their area on a regular basis so that teachers know when they will be coming in and can discuss children they may be worried about; others visit at the request of the school or when a child is formally referred to them. They are part of the LEA's Schools Psychological Service or Child Guidance Service, and are often based in a Child Guidance Clinic. A large proportion of their time is taken up with identifying and assessing children's special educational needs, especially under the new procedures introduced by the 1981 Education Act (see Chapter 3). Educational psychologists also work with children under school age who are likely to have special educational needs when they do start school, usually those children with a severe, or early-diagnosed, difficulty.

Education welfare officer (EWO) (also known as *education social worker*) Education welfare officers liaise with Social Services Departments and are responsible for the general well-being of school children, not only ensuring that they attend school regularly but also dealing with grants, allowances and services which they may need to be able to attend (e.g. clothing, transport, free school meals). The job involves a substantial amount of fieldwork, such as visiting families where there is a record of absence, lateness or other difficulties at school, and the Educational Welfare Service (staffed by the EWOs) is usually based in the community rather than the Town Hall, in a school or small area office. EWOs are also involved with the families of children who have special educational needs, and in some LEAs they deliver to parents the 'Section 5 Letter' which initiates the formal assessment procedure for such children (see Chapter 13).

Careers officer LEAs are obliged to set up a Careers Service, which is staffed by careers officers. As with education welfare officers, their job involves travelling in the community rather than being part of the central LEA administration, and so they also generally work in area teams based in a local school. Their job is part counselling, part provider of information. They liaise with secondary school careers teachers, and also with the employers in an area. There were over 4000 LEA careers officers in the

UK in 1985, of whom about a sixth were in government-funded posts dealing with unemployed young people and those on YTS.

Youth and community worker/officer   Although youth work has many of the functions of social work, it is primarily an education service. Most full-time, qualified youth and community workers (around 5000 of them in Britain in 1986) are employed by LEAs, although a few work for Social Services Departments. The vast majority of youth work, however, is still done by volunteers. Qualified youth and community workers generally have a teaching qualification; some institutions offer a BEd degree or postgraduate courses in youth and community studies. They are generally based in youth clubs and centres, and work on a variety of projects including those for the unemployed.

Schools–industry liaison officer (SILO)   They are appointed by LEAs to co-ordinate the work of schools and industry within their area.

School level

Headteacher   Virtually every school in the country has a headteacher who is responsible for the overall running of the school and for the rules, discipline and curriculum, under the guidance of the school's governors and subject to any requirements of the LEA and, since the 1988 Education Reform Act, to the national curriculum. While reducing headteachers' autonomy in curricular matters, the 1988 Act increases it in matters of financial management. The job requires management and interpersonal skills, but until recently heads received no special training. In 1983 the DES announced the setting up of a national training centre in Bristol for heads and senior staff. Headteachers' salaries are linked to the number of pupils in their school.

Deputy headteacher   The deputy head assists the head in the running of a school, often liaising between the head and the rest of the staff. Large secondary schools may have two or more deputy heads, with defined areas of responsibility (e.g. for the curriculum); primary schools normally have one. As with heads, their salaries are linked to the number of pupils in the school.

Class teacher   Class teachers are the main category of professionals involved in the education of children, and more detailed information about them is given in the next section. Usually one teacher works with a class of children, teaching a particular subject in the case of secondary schools, or teaching virtually all of the curriculum in the case of primary schools. Thus, children in a primary school will spend most of their time with the same teacher in any one year, while secondary school pupils will be taught by a variety of different teachers. A less common pattern is for teachers to combine classes and teach together ('team teaching'), usually for particular subjects or in open-plan primary schools.

Special school teacher   Teachers in special schools are paid an additional allowance, but the small size of the schools and the move towards integrating children with special needs into ordinary schools mean that they have fewer prospects for promotion than teachers in mainstream schools. They must be qualified teachers, and in Scotland must have previously taught in an ordinary school for at least a year (this is common practice but not compulsory in England and Wales). Teachers of the deaf, partially hearing and blind must in addition have a specialist qualification, and many other teachers in special schools (and increasingly in ordinary schools too) attend in-service training courses on children with special educational needs. With increasing integration, some special school teachers are spending part of their time in ordinary schools, supporting children with special educational needs in ordinary classes or special classes and units attached to the ordinary school.

Nursery school teacher   A nursery school teacher is a qualified teacher who usually specialises, during training, in the education of nursery and infant children. Nursery school teachers teach in either a nursery school or a special nursery class attached to a primary school, and are helped by nursery assistants and nursery students (doing the practical part of their training). In nursery schools and classes, in England in 1985, there were approximately 6000 qualified nursery teachers, 8000 nursery assistants, 3000 nursery students and 100 or so unqualified teacher's aides or helpers.

Nursery assistant   A nursery assistant is not qualified as a teacher, but holds a National Nursery Examination Board (NNEB) qualification (a theoretical and practical course studying the development and care of young children).

Teacher's aide   Also sometimes called an infant helper or primary helper, a teacher's aide is someone without formal teaching qualifications who works alongside the regular class teacher. The Plowden Report (see Chapter 3) recommended greater use of such posts, but they have never become common.

Welfare assistant   This is a person without teaching qualifications who is employed by the LEA to work alongside a class teacher, often with a particular child who has special educational needs. His or her job is to deal with the child's physical needs (e.g. arising from incontinence, lack of mobility or impaired speech) rather than to help teach the whole class.

Supply teacher   Each LEA has a supply of teachers who are sent in to schools to cover for absences of regular teaching staff. They may be attached to a particular school for a single day or even part of a day, or for a substantially longer period.

Peripatetic teacher   Some qualified teachers are not attached to a particular school but visit and work in several schools in an area, for instance teaching music or languages, or working with partially hearing children.

Home liaison teacher   In some LEAs there are qualified teachers whose job is to liaise between the school and the home, by visiting the child's family at home, seeing parents if they visit the school, and by organising activities, both during and after school hours, to encourage parental involvement with the school and with their children's education. They are most likely to be attached to primary schools in areas of social need, or to special schools.

Educational home visitor Some LEAs employ teachers to visit families with a pre-school child before they start school, usually for about an hour a week, to play with the child and involve the parents in finding out more about the child's development and needs. They perform a similar role to home liaison teachers in encouraging parental involvement in their children's education, but differ in working with children under five.

Home tutor A home tutor is a teacher employed to teach children at home when they are unable to attend school for any length of time, for instance because of illness.

Laboratory technician/assistant Laboratory technicians and assistants maintain laboratory and workshop equipment, usually in secondary schools or institutes of further or higher education. They provide technical assistance to teachers, especially in science subjects, and sometimes also deal with audio-visual equipment.

Audio-visual technician Audio-visual technicians are responsible for the operation and maintenance of audio-visual equipment. Some posts exist attached to a particular secondary school, especially a very large comprehensive, but most A-V technicians are appointed to a local authority centre, or work in further or higher education.

Media resources officer A few large authorities have created these posts, which involve not merely the operation and maintenance of audio-visual equipment and other educational technology, but also the preparation and production of audio-visual materials and the in-service training of teaching staff in the use of the equipment.

Ancillary staff All educational establishments are dependent for their day-to-day running on the ancillary staff. They include the administrative and clerical staff, who often work part-time, especially in primary schools: the secretaries, clerical assistants, typists, and (especially in private boarding schools) bursars, who are responsible for the school's financial and domestic management. Another group are the kitchen and canteen staff, responsible for providing school dinners. Their numbers have decreased since 1980, when responsibility for the provision of school meals was delegated to LEAs, with a legal obligation to provide meals only to children in families receiving Supplementary Benefit or Family Income Supplement. The other main category of ancillary staff can be described as premises-related: they include caretakers, cleaners, porters, gardeners and security staff.

(C) The teaching profession

Salaries and conditions

In 1987, the Teachers' Pay and Conditions Act abolished the existing salary
scales (see the introduction to Figures 7.5–7.8 below), and also the
Burnham Committees, in which representatives from the teachers' unions,
the LEAs and the DES had negotiated salary structure, levels of pay and
conditions of service. Instead, at least for the moment, new salary
structure, pay levels, and conditions of service are decided by the Secretary
of State. For the longer term, the Secretary of State proposes to replace the
Burnham Committees by a Teachers' Negotiating Group, with central
government rather than LEAs in a majority on the employers' side. Its
decisions would have to be accepted by a majority of both the employers'
and the teachers' representatives, but the government would retain the
right to impose a settlement in the case of a deadlock.

The present salary structure consists of a single 'standard scale' for all
qualified teachers except headteachers and deputy headteachers (ranging
from £9000 to £16,002 in 1991) plus five levels of 'incentive allowances'
(ranging from £927 to £5502). Heads' salaries range from £18,900 to
£40,002; deputy heads' from £18,300 to £29,100.

The new conditions of service spell out much more explicitly and exhaus-
tively than ever before the duties, and the working time, of teachers at all
levels. The duties include the following. Teachers are required to plan and
prepare lessons, assess and keep records of pupils' progress, and maintain
discipline. They are to engage in appraisal of their own work, and attend
in-service training. They must communicate with parents and others
outside school, and attend meetings where necessary. They must provide
cover for absent colleagues for up to three days, though this can be
extended for a teacher whose *classroom teaching* duties occupy less than
three-quarters of his or her working week, or where it is not 'reasonably
practical' for a supply teacher to be found to replace the absent colleague.

A teacher's working year is to consist of 1265 hours, spread reasonably
over 195 working days. (This does not include travelling time to and from
school.) In addition, teachers must work such extra hours as are needed to
fulfil their professional duties, for example in preparing lessons and
marking pupils' written work. Teachers are entitled to a reasonable
mid-day break, and do not have to supervise pupils during this period as
part of their normal duties. Of their annual working days, five are to be
allocated to in-service training (DES, 1990).

In recent years, teachers' salaries have fallen behind those of other
non-manual workers. Between 1975 and 1986, teachers' pay rose by 194%,
on average, compared with an average rise of 259% for all non-manual
earnings (New Society Database, 1986).

FACT

Approximately 520,000 full-time teachers were employed in schools in the UK in 1987–8 (9% below the peak level reached in 1979). Of these, 92% taught in maintained schools (48% in secondary, 39% in primary and 4% in special schools) and the remaining 8% taught in the private sector (Central Statistical Office, 1990, Table 3.30).

Women outnumber men in the teaching profession, making up over three-quarters of the teachers in primary schools, and just under half of the teachers in secondary schools. They are particularly over-represented as teachers of the youngest children. Figure 7.2 shows that as the age of the pupil increases, so the proportion of women teachers decreases.

Until October 1987 (see above) teaching posts were graded from scale 1 (the lowest) to scale 4, followed by senior teacher, deputy head and head. Although the precise categories no longer apply, the last published statistics to use them (1985) still illustrate the career possibilities for teachers in primary and secondary education, as Figures 7.3–7.5 show.

In both primary and secondary schools, women were more likely to be found at the bottom of the hierarchy of teaching posts. Figure 7.3 shows the women and the men on each scale as percentages of all teachers on that scale. Figures 7.4 and 7.5 show the women and men on each scale as percentages of all the women and of all the men in the teaching profession. (Primary and secondary schools are shown separately.)

The proportion of heads (and, therefore, the chance of becoming one) was higher in primary education, where schools were much smaller, but there

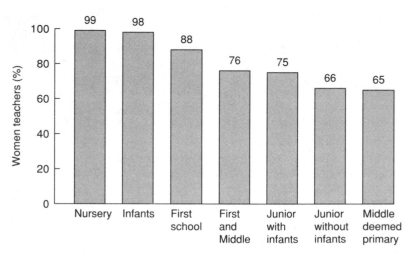

Figure 7.2   Percentages of women teachers in different types of primary school, England and Wales 1985
(Adapted from DES, 1985b)

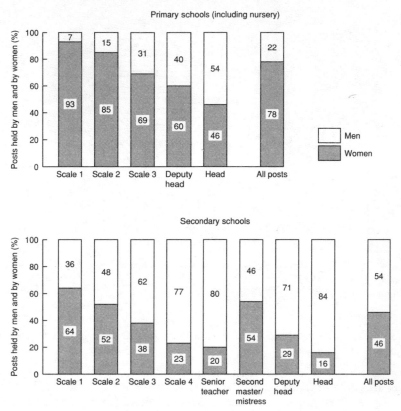

Figure 7.3   Percentages of each scale post held by men and by women, England and Wales 1985
(Adapted from DES, 1985b, Table B129)

were hardly any senior teachers or scale 4 posts. Secondary schools offered more rungs on the career ladder, but the chance of becoming a head-teacher was much lower. Differences between the sexes were very notice-able. Particularly striking were the much higher percentage of men than of women who were heads, and the much higher percentage of women than of men who were on the lowest two scales. These discrepancies existed in both the primary and the secondary sectors, but were especially marked in the primary.

Ethnic minorities are under-represented in the teaching profession in comparison with their numbers in the population. In eight LEAs surveyed in 1987 by the Commission for Racial Equality, the overall percentage of teachers who were from ethnic minorities was 2% (Ranger, 1988); the percentage of the total population of these LEAs who are from ethnic minorities is about 8.5% (OPCS, 1982. However, the latter figure is based on answers to a question in the 1981 census about the country of birth of

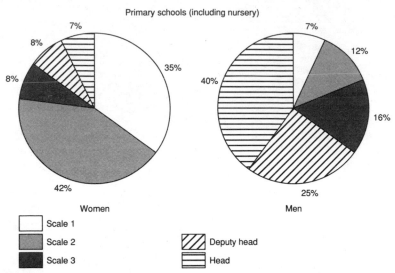

Figure 7.4   Percentages of men and of women teachers in each scale post, primary schools, England 1985
(Adapted from DES, 1985b, Table B129)

one's head of household, and cannot be considered very accurate. See Chapter 2).

Teachers from ethnic minorities are more likely to be found in junior posts than are white teachers: in 1987 (before the abolition of salary scales), 78% of ethnic minority teachers were on scales 1 and 2 (the lowest), compared with 57% of white teachers. Ethnic minority teachers are twice as likely as white teachers to be teaching subjects in which there is a shortage of teachers (Ranger, 1988).

Since 1984, all new teachers entering the profession in England and Wales must have a degree plus postgraduate teacher training if their first degree is not a BEd. The only exception (in 1987) was for people with suitable qualifications and some practical experience in craft, design and technology, a subject with teacher shortages. Graduates who obtained their degrees before January 1974 can teach in secondary schools without having taken a course of professional training, and those who graduated before January 1970 may teach in primary and special schools as well. In Scotland, all primary school teachers must have a degree, and so must all secondary school teachers except those teaching subjects such as music, PE or drama, for whom a college diploma is sufficient. However, in September 1988, the Secretary of State for Education announced proposals to allow certain people with no teaching training to become 'licensed teachers' at the discretion of local employers. These people would need to have qualifications and experience outside the education system in subjects for which there is a shortage of teachers. They would receive some form of 'on-the-job' training and, after successfully completing two years of

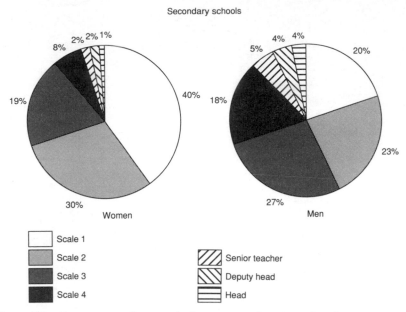

Figure 7.5   Percentages of men and of women teachers in each scale post, secondary schools, England 1985
(Adapted from DES, 1985b, Table B129)

teaching, could become fully qualified as teachers. Similar conditions would apply to people with teaching qualifications from abroad that had not previously been recognised.

In 1985, 11,358 students enrolled on teacher training courses, just under a third (32%) of them in universities and the rest in public sector higher education, i.e. polytechnics and colleges (see Figure 7.6). This was 5% below the government's planned intake, mostly because of an under-recruitment of those planning to teach in secondary schools. Recruitment in some subjects such as mathematics fell 32% short of the government's targets.

The proportion of the teaching force who have degrees has been steadily increasing (see Figure 7.7).

It is higher among men than women, with the lowest proportion of graduates teaching in primary schools and the highest in non-maintained schools (see Figure 7.8).

An important aspect of the teacher's job is the size of the class he or she is expected to teach (on average, this is greater than the pupil/teacher ratio, as calculations of the latter include staff who do little or no classroom teaching). Primary classes are generally larger than classes in secondary schools. (For data on the pupil/teacher ratio and class size, see Chapter 5, Figures 5.8 and 5.12.)

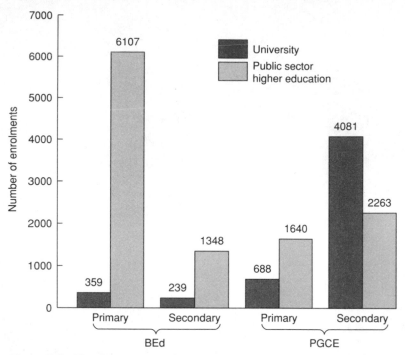

Figure 7.6   Enrolments on teacher training courses, England and Wales 1985 (Great Britain for universities)
(Adapted from DES, 1985a, Table 12)

Many teachers belong to one or more teaching unions. Overlapping membership and the inclusion in some membership figures of non-teaching members make it difficult to express union membership as a percentage of the teaching profession. Figure 7.9 shows the membership figures issued in 1988 by the main teaching unions; the total membership of all eight is greater than the total number of teachers (*Education Guardian*, 1988).

(D) Teaching staff in further and higher education

FACT

In 1988–9, local authorities in England employed 64,000 academic staff in further education, and 26,000 in higher education (in colleges and polytechnics now mostly removed to the PCFC sector). Universities (in Great Britain) employed 46,000 academic staff (HM Treasury, 1990, Tables 11.11 and 11.13).

Men far outnumber women in further and higher education teaching, especially in senior posts. In 1988–9, there were four men to every woman at lecturer level, 11 men to every woman at senior lecturer level, and 31

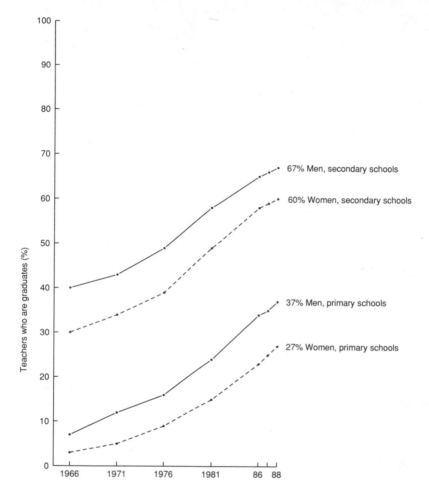

Figure 7.7   Percentages of men and women teachers who are graduates, in primary and secondary schools, United Kingdom 1966–88
(Adapted from Government Statistical Service, 1989, Table 9)

men to every woman at the level of professor in British universities (see Figure 7.10). The discrepancy is particularly great in the physical sciences and mathematics, where male lecturers outnumber female by ten to one, and male professors outnumber female by a hundred to one.

Career structure
Most academic teaching posts in universities (but not public sector higher education) have traditionally been offered on a 'tenured' basis, so that academic staff can lose their job only on grounds of professional misconduct (and not on such grounds as redundancy or financial exigency). However, under the 1988 Education Reform Act no new tenured appoint-

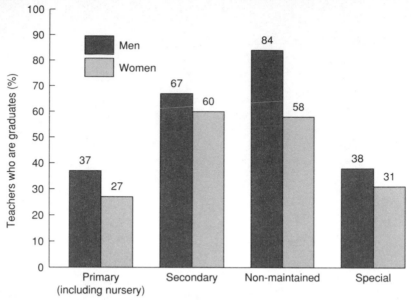

Figure 7.8   Percentages of men and women teachers who are graduates, in different types of schools, United Kingdom 1987–8
(Adapted from Government Statistical Service, 1989, Table 9)

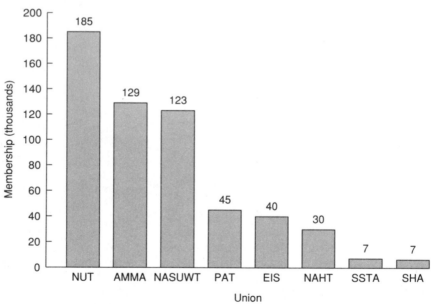

Figure 7.9   Membership of main teachers' unions, 1988
(Adapted from Education Guardian, 1988)
Key: NUT — National Union of Teachers; AMMA — Assistant Masters and Mistresses Association; PAT — Professional Association of Teachers; EIS — Educational Institute of Scotland; NAHT— National Association of Head Teachers; SSTA — Scottish Secondary Teachers Association; SHA — Secondary Heads Association

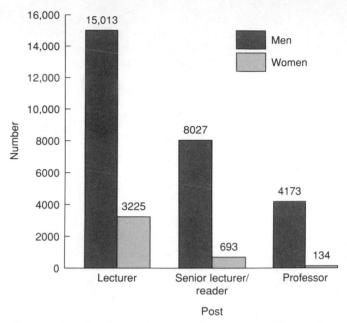

Figure 7.10   Numbers of men and women teaching staff in universities, Great Britain 1988–9
(Adapted from Universities Funding Council, 1989, Vol. 1, Table 29)

ments can be made. Academics already in post retain their tenure only so long as they do not move to another university or accept promotion within their present university.

The main academic posts within universities are typically as described below, though there is a great deal of variation between universities.

Chancellor   The chancellor is the titular head of a university, with a purely ceremonial function, notably in conferring degrees. He or she is usually a well-known public figure, who need not have any connection with the academic world (such as a member of the Royal Family). In the ancient Scottish universities, the chancellor is elected by the graduates.

Pro chancellor   Nominally a deputy to the chancellor (for whom he or she does sometimes stand in on ceremonial occasions, such as graduation ceremonies), the pro chancellor does have a substantial role, as chair of the council of a university, with overall responsibility for its financial and other non-academic affairs. It is usually a part-time appointment, often held by people distinguished in the world outside university, such as lawyers and business people.

Vice chancellor (VC)   Again, the vice chancellor is nominally a deputy to the chancellor, but in reality is the chief academic and administrative officer of a university, in charge of its day-to-day running (though he or she does also stand in for the chancellor on ceremonial occasions). He or she controls and co-ordinates the activities of committees and planning boards, oversees the working of academic departments and liaises with outside bodies. This is a full-time appointment, and in most universities a permanent one, though some (notably Oxford, Cambridge and London) elect their vice chancellor for a period of several years at a time.

Principal   The chief academic and administrative officer of a Scottish university, he or she is usually styled 'principal and vice chancellor', the latter title used when standing in for the chancellor on ceremonial occasions. (The University of London has both a principal and a vice chancellor.)

Pro vice chancellor   Some universities now have deputy or pro vice chancellors, who chair major committees and stand in for the vice chancellor. These posts are often held for a limited term by senior academic members of the university.

Rector   A rector is the chair of the university court (the main finance committee) of one of the ancient Scottish universities. Elected by the students for a term of several years, rectors have been less exclusively drawn than most other senior officers of universities from 'establishment' circles: they have included a communist trade union leader and several television personalities, such as Malcolm Muggeridge, John Cleese and Muriel Gray. Most treat the position as purely ceremonial, but they can actively preside over their courts' proceedings if they choose, and in recent years a few have done so.

Master   A traditional title for the head of a college in Oxford and Cambridge Universities (and occasionally elsewhere).

Dean   A dean is the head of a faculty, such as a faculty of science, or a faculty of arts. A deanship may be a permanent appointment, or a temporary one held for a limited term by senior academic members of the faculty. The duties and powers of deans vary from university to university.

Professor   This is the highest purely academic appointment. Professors are responsible for conducting and promoting teaching and research in their subjects. A post as professor — known for historical reasons as a 'chair' — may be *established* or *personal*. An established chair is a permanent post in a university: when one occupant leaves it, another will normally be appointed in his or her place. A personal chair is conferred on a particular individual, usually for distinguished scholarship, research and published work, and continues only as long as his or her academic career. Traditionally, professors were the heads of academic departments. Often they still are, but in recent years it has become common for other senior academics to act as heads of departments, sometimes in rotation.

Reader   A reader engages in teaching and research. Like a personal chair, a readership is usually conferred on an individual for merit in scholarship, research and published work. In status, it lies between a professorship and a senior lectureship, but is equivalent to the latter in duties (and salary scale).

Senior lecturer   A senior lecturer engages in teaching and research. The criteria for promotion from lecturer are not clearly defined, but are generally concerned with qualities in teaching, research and, sometimes, administration. There is no sharp division of duties between senior lecturer and lecturer, but a senior lecturer is, in general, more likely than a lecturer to hold such posts as dean or head of department, or to chair university committees.

Lecturer   Lecturers engage in teaching and research. Despite their title, lecturers' teaching does not consist only, or even mainly, of giving lectures. They also hold tutorials and seminars, and comment on students' written work, as well as setting and marking examinations. (Lecturers at the Open University do not normally give lectures at all; they produce correspondence material for their students, as well as working with BBC colleagues on the production of radio and television programmes.) Most universities have no formal qualifications for the post of lecturer, but in practice lecturers almost always have a good honours degree, and usually a higher degree and research experience in their subject.

In addition, there are sometimes temporary posts such as 'teaching fellow' or 'tutorial assistant', which are available for a limited period.

As well as the academic posts above, which carry responsibilities for both teaching and research, universities also have posts with research duties alone. Research posts often have short-term contracts and are rarely held on a tenured basis. They are increasingly being funded by external sources, such as industry. Definitions of different levels of appointment are varied and sometimes imprecise, but two broad levels can be distinguished:

Research fellow or *research officer*   People who hold these posts are deemed able to carry out research without supervision. They generally have a higher degree.

Research associate or *research assistant*   The work of research associates and assistants is carried out under supervision, sometimes as part of a research team. They are often allowed (and expected) to spend part of their time studying for a higher degree.

Public sector higher education institutions (such as polytechnics) have a similar, though not identical hierarchy of posts, but they are too recently established to have acquired the more colourful historic positions and titles of the universities. The head of a public sector institution is usually called the director or principal. Directors are usually assisted by deputies, though sometimes by pro-directors: generally, the former are permanent appointments, the latter temporary appointments from among senior academic staff in rotation.

The most senior post is usually principal lecturer (though some polytechnics have professors); the other posts are senior lecturer, lecturer grade II and lecturer grade I. The ratio of more-senior to more-junior posts allowed in a college depends on the proportions of advanced and less-advanced courses it teaches.

Sources and further reading

CIPFA (no single date) *Financial Information Services*, Vol. 20, *Education*, London, Chartered Institute of Public Finance and Accountancy.

CIPFA (1989) *Local Government Trends 1989*, London, Chartered Institute of Public Finance and Accountancy.

CSO (1990) *Social Trends*, No. 20, 1990 edn, London, HMSO.

DES (1985a) *Annual Report 1985*, London, Department of Education and Science.

DES (1985b) *Statistics of Education: Teachers in Service 1985*, London, Department of Education and Science.

DES (1990) *School Teachers' Pay and Conditions Document 1990*, London, HMSO.

Education Guardian (1988) Untitled news item, *Guardian*, 4 April 1988.

Gordon, P. and Lawton, D. (1984) *A Guide to English Educational Terms*, London, Batsford.

Government Statistical Service (1989) *Educational Statistics for the United Kingdom 1989*, London, HMSO.

New Society Database (1986) Teachers' pay, *New Society*, 31 October 1986.

OPCS (1982) *Census 1981: County Reports*, London, HMSO.

Ranger, C. (1988) *Ethnic Minority Teachers*, London, Commission for Racial Equality.

Rowntree, D. (1981) *A Dictionary of Education*, London, Harper & Row.

Universities Funding Council (1989) *University Statistics 1988–89*, London, Universities' Statistical Record.

CHAPTER 8   FINANCE AND RESOURCES

England and Wales

As this edition of *The Education Fact File* goes to press (late 1990), the government, local authorities, schools and colleges are in the throes of implementing radical changes to the way education is financed and managed. These changes stem mainly from three Acts of Parliament. First, the *1988 Education Reform Act* transfers many financial and managerial responsibilities from local education authorities to all but the smallest schools and colleges. Secondly, the *1988 Local Government Finance Act* replaced domestic rates by the Community Charge (or 'poll tax'), and business rates by the National Non-domestic Rate (or 'uniform business rate'). Finally, the *1989 Local Government and Housing Act* introduced a new system for financing and controlling local authorities' capital expenditure. In the first edition of the *Fact File*, we gave a detailed description of the system as it operated before these changes. No such account of the new system in operation is yet possible. In Part 1 below, we outline what is proposed and beginning to happen under it. But inevitably, our statistical data, and our descriptions of how money has been raised and spent in recent years, almost all apply to the old system. The resignation of Mrs Thatcher while the *Fact File* is in press adds an extra uncertainty, especially to the future of the Community Charge.

Part 1   Where the money comes from

The financing of education is shared between central and local government. Most of central government's contribution is indirect, consisting of grants to local authorities. Its direct expenditure is mainly for higher education and science. The local authorities' educational expenditure forms about 40% of their total expenditure; it is mainly on schools.

FACT

In 1989–90, central government's direct expenditure on education amounted to just over £4 billion, of which about 70% was for universities, polytechnics and other colleges of higher education, and 18% for science. Local authorities' expenditure on education amounted to £17 billion, 74% of it on schools and approximately 10% on further education (HM Treasury, 1990, Tables 11.1–2, 15.2, 16.1–2 and 21.4.8–9).

As the 1988 Education Reform Act comes into effect, the local authorities' share of educational expenditure is diminishing and will probably continue to diminish, though it is impossible to predict by how much. Under the terms of the Act, polytechnics and certain other colleges of higher education are now removed entirely from the control of LEAs, and are financed directly by central government — as are Grant Maintained Schools. As yet, these schools account for only a small amount of annual expenditure — £3 million in 1989–90 — but the government's expenditure plans provide for this sum to increase (to £20 million by 1991–2) as more schools choose to 'opt out' of LEA control and financing (HM Treasury, 1990, Table 11.1). In addition, the Act will reduce the local authorities' control even over those educational functions and services that they continue to finance, as Local Management of Schools comes into operation (see below).

Local government finance

Under the 1988 Local Government Finance Act, the local authorities' money now comes from three main sources. The first is the local community, through the Community Charge, which is payable by almost every adult (some 35 million in all, as against 17 million who paid rates), and the level of which is set by each local authority (though subject to 'capping' by central government). The second is central government, mainly in the form of a Revenue Support Grant (RSG). The third lies somewhere in between local and national revenue: the National Non-domestic Rate, which replaces the business rate, but the level of which is set nationally and the proceeds of which are pooled nationally (separately for England and Wales) and distributed to local authorities in proportion to their populations. A small amount of money is also raised through fees and other charges, but this income is insignificant as a proportion of expenditure in the education service, unlike other services such as housing.

FACT

About half of local authority expenditure in the United Kingdom is financed by central government grants (49% in 1989–90); the rest is revenue raised by local authorities themselves. In 1989–90, 38% of local authority expenditure was financed from domestic and business rates, and the remaining 13% from local authorities' surpluses on trading, rents and borrowing (HM Treasury, 1990, Table 21.4.13).

The government's declared intention in introducing the Act is to make the processes of raising revenue and financial planning simpler and more 'transparent' than before, and thus to make local authorities more account-able to their voters for their spending. Before the start of each year, the government is to assess the amount of expenditure it considers that each authority will require in order to provide a standard level of services. This takes into account the particular needs of the authority: some areas will have particularly high numbers of old people, for instance, or underpri-vileged groups, or bad housing, which require higher spending for the same level of services. Then, taking into account the resources of the authority, and the revenue available to it from the National Non-domestic Rate, the government is to decide how much Revenue Support Grant it will give, and how much revenue it considers should be raised by the authority itself through Community Charge.

However, a local authority is to decide its own level of Community Charge; it is not committed to following the government's recommendation. Of all the main sources of finance, only the level of Community Charge is within the control of the local authorities. Thus, any decision by an authority to spend more or less on services than the government's assumed level will be reflected directly in the level of charge it has to set. According to the government, this will improve accountability of local authorities to their electorate (HM Treasury, 1990, Chapter 21, Para. 4.7; CIPFA, 1989, Chapter 2).

In the years before the 1988 Act, the government introduced elaborate procedures to control the spending of local authorities, initially by financially penalising those authorities that exceeded the amount the government thought they should spend, and ultimately by imposing limits on the amount of revenue a recalcitrant authority could raise ('rate capping'). This was necessary, the government argued, because the local authorities were not effectively accountable to anyone for their spending, as their rate-payers formed too small a proportion of their electorate. Under the new system, such controls should not be so necessary. Nevertheless, the Secretary of State for the Environment is empowered to 'charge cap' local authorities, either by setting a universal limit or by singling out those authorities whose levels of Community Charge he or she considers excessive. In 1990–1, the first year of operation of the new system, he followed the latter course, and capped the charges set by 21 authorities.

Local management of schools
Under the terms of the 1988 Education Reform Act, the LEAs will continue (subject to such constraints as charge capping) to set the overall, authority-wide budget for schools under their control (known as the 'general schools budget'). But thereafter, the powers of LEAs are now to be greatly restricted.

First, they will be required to distribute most (possibly around three-quarters) of these funds (the 'aggregated schools budget') between schools strictly and even-handedly according to a formula, to be devised by each LEA but requiring approval by the DES. An acceptable formula will probably be expected to make each school's 'budget share' depend mainly on the numbers of pupils in the school, but also to take into account such factors as the ages of the children, the subjects they are studying, and the numbers with special needs; and also perhaps the levels of social advantage and disadvantage in the community the school serves. The intention is that an LEA will not be able to favour particular schools, or to use the granting and withholding of funds as a means of enforcing policies, or of promoting some educational practices and discouraging others (except to a marginal extent with some limited discretionary funds that can be kept outside the aggregated budget). However, the DES has expressed a willingness to look sympathetically at limited transitional arrangements to help schools that enter the new system with serious inherited problems, such as buildings in a very poor state of repair.

Secondly, the LEAs will be required to delegate many of their responsibilities for the management and control of the schools' budget share, and for the appointment and dismissal of staff, to the governing bodies of the schools (and of the larger colleges that remain under LEA control). The members of a governing body may in their turn delegate most of these responsibilities to the head teacher, or they may choose to discharge them themselves. In either case, decisions about spending priorities — e.g. on staffing as against computers, or educational visits as against redecoration — and about the hiring and firing of teachers, will now be made at the level of the school itself, not by the LEA.

This new system, now known as the Local Management of Schools (LMS), began to operate on 1 April 1990, and is planned to be completely in operation by April 1993. As with most of their changes to local authorities' funding, the government's aim for LMS is increased accountability, and therefore efficiency. A school's funding now depends above all on its pupil numbers, and open enrolment under the 1988 Act (see Chapter 4) allows parents much wider choice of school for their children to attend. Schools will therefore be liable to lose pupils and funds if they fail to satisfy parents. This, the government believes, will make schools more directly and effectively accountable to parents, and more responsive to their criticisms and wishes. As we go to press, however, LEAs are still drawing up their formulae and submitting them to the DES for approval. It is too early to discover what the effects of the new system in practice will be.

Capital expenditure
Spending by both central and local government is of two types: current and capital. Current expenditure covers day-to-day items such as salaries and services; capital expenditure covers items with a longer term use, such as buildings and machinery. About 96% of local authorities' educational expenditure in 1989–90 was current, and 4% capital.

The amount that local authorities can raise and spend on capital items is subject to controls by central government. Here, too, a new system has recently been introduced, this time in the 1989 Local Government and Housing Act. Under this system, the government will still control the total capital expenditure of local authorities, but now intends to allow the authorities almost complete freedom to decide their own priorities within that overall sum. Local authorities now have four main sources of funds for capital expenditure: *borrowing*, which is subject to approval by central government; *capital grants*, also from central government, which will specify the purposes for which they are to be used, and the amount the local authority must itself contribute; *capital receipts*, from the sale of assets such as land and council houses, though the local authorities must first set aside 50% of these receipts (75% in the case of council house sales) towards repaying their debts; and *ordinary revenue* from the Community Charge, etc., for which the government assumes the local authorities to be accountable to their voters (CIPFA, 1990, Chapter 20.3; HM Treasury, 1990, Chapter 21, Paras. 4.8–4.10).

Direct government funding
In addition to its indirect funding of schools through local authorities, and

its direct funding of higher education, the government provides some direct funding for education through various departments in addition to the Department of Education and Science and the Welsh Office — the Home Office, the Department of the Environment and the Department of Employment.

In 1984, the Education (Grants and Awards) Act was passed to enable the DES to allocate directly a small proportion (up to 1%) of the Block Grant to support specific educational projects which the Secretary of State judged to be particularly important; a grant could cover either 50% or 70% of the costs of a project (60% from 1990–91). These Education Support Grants (ESGs) were first offered to local authorities in England and Wales in 1985–6, for 12 areas including science teaching in primary schools, maths teaching generally, and the provision of micros for children with special educational needs; the total central government expenditure was £10 million. Four new areas were added in 1986–7, including training for school governors, and education about the misuse of drugs; and central government expenditure rose to £34 million. By 1989–90, the government's grants had risen to £82 million to support expenditure on 15 'activities of national priority', with LEAs encouraged to seek additional funding from outside the public sector. In 1989–90, just over half of ESG funds were devoted to projects concerned with the local management of schools and the national curriculum. All but a handful of LEAs bid for these grants (HM Treasury, 1990, Table 11.1; CIPFA, 1989, p. 18).

Under Section 11 of the 1966 Local Government Act, local authorities can apply to the Home Office for 75% of the costs of employing extra staff for educational (and other) purposes in areas with large numbers of Commonwealth immigrants for whom special provision is required because of differences in languages or customs. In 1985–6, an estimated £71 million of 'Section 11 money' was allocated to education (CIPFA, 1988, Chapter 2).

Some local authorities also receive direct government grants from the Department of the Environment under the Urban Programme, which provides 75% of the funding for projects in deprived areas. The first phase of the Urban Programme concentrated mainly on educational provision, following the Plowden Report (see Chapter 3 above), and was used to provide extra nursery education, day nurseries, community centres and language classes for immigrants.

Much of the responsibility for education and training related to employment rests with the Training, Enterprise and Education Division (formerly the Training Agency) of the Department of Employment. Its main current training projects (see Chapter 12), and their budgets for 1989–90 are:

- *Employment Training (ET)* — £1112 million;

- the *Youth Training Scheme (YTS)* — £1010 million;

- the *Technical and Vocational Education Initiative (TVEI)* — £117 million;

- *Work-related Further Education (WRFE)* — £112 million.

The Training Agency's total spending on its main training programmes in 1989–90 was £2481 million (HM Treasury, 1990, Tables 6.3–6.11).

Funding of higher education
Universities have always had a considerable degree of financial autonomy, being funded (apart from the Open University) by central government on the recommendation of an independent body, now the Universities Funding Council (UFC). The funding of non-university higher education (i.e. polytechnics and colleges of higher education) now gives them similar autonomy, having been transferred by the 1988 Education Reform Act from local authority to central government responsibility, with a Polytechnics and Colleges Funding Council (PCFC) parallel to the UFC. Local authorities in England and Wales remain responsible for student grants, and thus for that portion of university, polytechnic and college funding that comes from students' tuition fees.

In 1989–90, the UFC received £1.9 billion and the PCFC £1.1 billion in government funds. In addition, the government provided £158 million for institutions of higher education outside the auspices of these funding councils, notably the Open University, Cranfield Institute of Technology and the Royal College of Art. Local authorities paid a further £1.1 billion in mandatory and discretionary student awards (HM Treasury, 1990, Tables 11.1 and 11.2).

From 1990–1, however, the government proposes to alter the balance between these methods of finance, more than doubling the tuition fees and correspondingly reducing the direct funding of higher education institutions. The fees are payable by local authorities, who will be reimbursed for their extra expenditure. This change is intended to improve the performance of the institutions, by making their funding depend more on their ability to attract students in competition with one another.

Also from 1990–1, the government is to introduce a new system of student loans to supplement grants. The grants will initially be frozen at their present level, while the loans will rise in line with inflation until they reach the level of the grant. Then the two will be kept equal, and allowed to rise together in line with inflation. A loan will be repayable when the student's earnings reach a level of 85% of the national average wage, and a period of 5 to 10 years allowed for the repayment (CIPFA, 1989, p. 17).

In-service training of teachers
Since April 1987, the in-service training of teachers (and others, such as youth workers) has been organised and financed under what is officially termed the Local Education Authorities Training Grants Scheme (LEATGS). Under the scheme, the Secretary of State each year defines a number of 'national priority areas' for in-service training. LEAs submit their in-service training plans to him or her for approval. These plans may propose training programmes in either the national priority areas, or in areas considered by an LEA to be of local priority. If the plans are approved, the DES gives grants of 70% of the cost of national priority training programmes (65% from 1990–1), and 50% of the cost of local priority programmes. In 1989–90, payments under the scheme amounted to £130 million (HM Treasury, 1990, Table 11.1).

Unofficial parental contributions
In addition to their official funding, a number of schools receive cash payments and other gifts from parents of their pupils. These contributions are not shown in official statistics of educational expenditure, but in 1990 an attempt was made to quantify them by the *Mail on Sunday*, which commissioned a survey of a representative sample of primary schools by the National Foundation for Educational Research. Overall, the researchers estimate, parents contribute some £40 million per annum to primary schools in England and Wales. But this total sum is distributed very unevenly among the schools. At one extreme, 6% of primary schools receive less than £1 per child, and a further 21% less than £5; at the other extreme, 3% of schools receive over £50 per child and 0.2% over £100. (The highest figure found for an individual school was £248 per child.) In about 13% of schools, the money contributed by parents amounts to more than the schools' official funding from their LEAs.

Of this money, 18% is spent on computers — the largest single item of expenditure. A further 14% is spent on books, and other major items are educational visits, decoration and maintenance, science equipment and schools furniture (Lightfoot, 1990).

Part 2   Where the money goes

Overall spending on education
Education is one of the largest consumers of public money: the total expenditure on education in 1989–90 by central and local government in the United Kingdom was an estimated £24.1 billion, some 14% of the total spending on all services. Only Social Security and Health had more spent on them (HM Treasury, 1990, Tables 21.2.9 and 29.2.12). Figure 8.1 shows for the United Kingdom the estimated public expenditure for 1989–90 on the highest spending services.

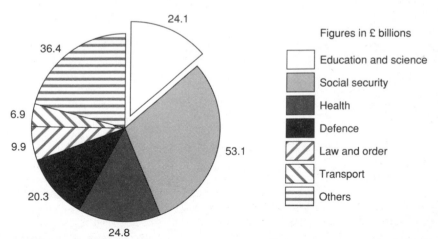

Figures in £ billions

- Education and science
- Social security
- Health
- Defence
- Law and order
- Transport
- Others

Figure 8.1   Estimated public expenditure on major services, United Kingdom 1989–90
(Adapted from HM Treasury, 1990, Table 21.2.9)

Within the education service, expenditure in 1989–90 planned by the DES (most of it actually spent by LEAs) is divided as shown in Figure 8.2.

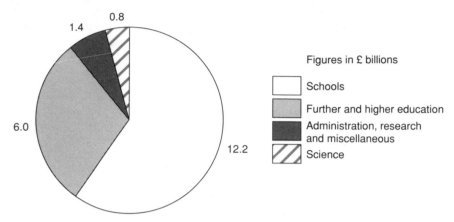

Figure 8.1   DES and English LEA spending, 1989–90
(Adapted from HM Treasury, 1990, Tables 11.1 and 11.2)
Note: These figures refer to spending on science in the United Kingdom; universities in Great Britain; mandatory awards in England and Wales; and schools, polytechnics and colleges in England

Of the £12.2 billion (60%) spent on schools, nearly all (£11.5 billion) is current expenditure by LEAs. This is divided as shown in Figure 8.3.

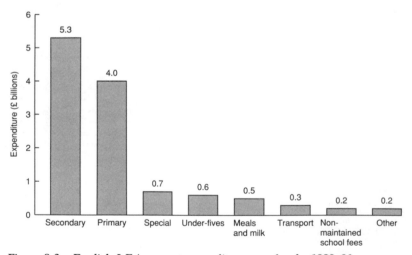

Figure 8.3   English LEA current expenditure on schools, 1989–90
(Adapted from HM Treasury, 1990, Table 11.2)

Of the £6.0 billion (30%) spent on further and higher eduation, nearly all (£5.7 billion) is current expenditure by both central government and

LEAs, the former mainly on higher education, the latter largely on further education. The amounts spent on the main sectors are shown in Figure 8.4.

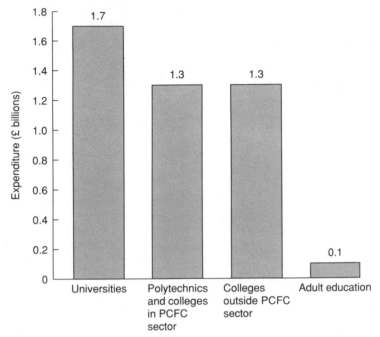

Figure 8.4   DES and English LEA current expenditure on further and higher education, 1989–90 (excluding student grants and loans)
(Adapted from HM Treasury, 1990, Tables 11.1 and 11.2)

Taking all sectors together, LEA recurrent expenditure is divided among various categories as shown in Figure 8.5.

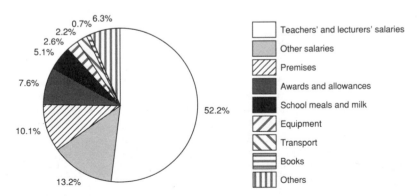

Figure 8.5   Percentage of LEA recurrent expenditure in major categories, England 1985–6
(Adapted from DES, 1987, Chart 2)

Trends over time in overall spending

Expenditure on education has increased steadily over the last few years, even in 'real terms' after inflation is taken into account, as Figure 8.6 shows.

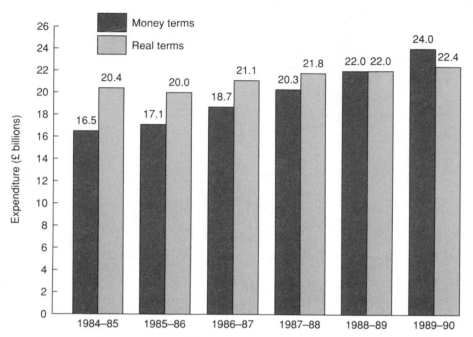

Figure 8.6   Total expenditure on education by central and local government 1984–5 to 1989–90, in money terms and real terms
(Adapted from HM Treasury, 1990, Tables 21.2.4, 21.2.5 and 21.2.9)
Note: The 'real terms' figures are expressed in 1988–9 values

However, as a percentage of total government expenditure, spending on education fell during the 1980s, as Figure 8.7 shows. Educational spending also declined in the 1980s as a percentage of the gross domestic product (GDP) — from 5.5% of the United Kingdom GDP in 1980–1 to 4.9% in 1986–7 (DES, 1989, Table 9).

Expenditure per pupil

Educational expenditure is often expressed in terms of the amount spent per pupil or student. This figure is known as the 'unit cost', and is arrived at simply by dividing the total amount spent on a service (e.g. nursery schools) by the number of children using it (expressed as 'full-time equivalents', so that two part-time children would count as one full-time equivalent). Unit costs vary considerably between different sectors of the education system, as is shown by Figures 8.8 (schools) and 8.9 (further and higher education).

Unit costs may be broken down further into the amount spent on teachers, books and equipment, ancillary staff, transport, and so on. Teachers' salaries account for the largest proportion of education spending in all

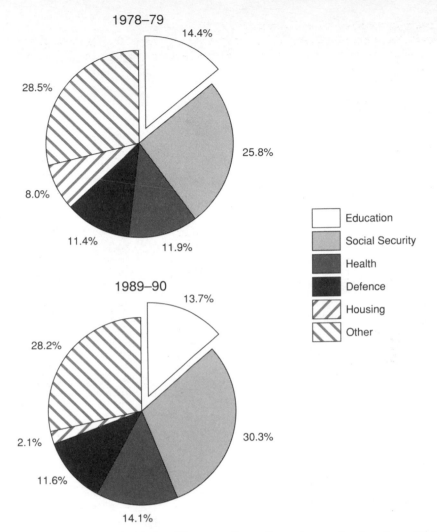

Figure 8.7   Percentage of public expenditure devoted to major functions, United Kingdom, 1978–9 and 1989–90 (Adapted from HM Treasury, 1988, Vol. 1, Chart 1.10; 1990, Table 21.2.9)

types of school, though this varies from around 70% in primary and secondary schools to 59% in special schools. This is mainly because the wages of education support staff (such as nursery assistants and welfare assistants) and other non-teaching staff figure much more prominently in the spending of special schools (27%) than they do in the spending of primary (14%) or secondary (11%) schools. The way the costs break down is affected by the region as well as the type of school: in rural areas, for instance, transport costs will account for a higher proportion of spending than in metropolitan areas (CIPFA, 1990, Tables 1, 2 and 3. Note: Here 'primary' includes nursery schools).

Regional variations in expenditure per pupil   There is considerable varia-

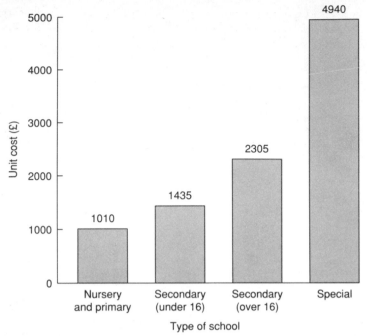

Figure 8.8   Unit costs (per pupil per annum) of schooling, England 1987–8
(Adapted from CIPFA, 1990, Table 7)
Note: These figures include direct and indirect costs of providing tuition, but exclude
costs of transport, school meals and milk, central administration and financing of
capital expenditure

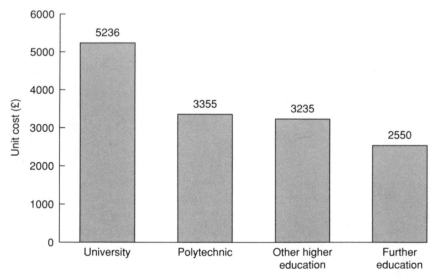

Figure 8.9   Unit costs (per student per annum) of further and higher education,
England 1987–8
(Adapted from CIPFA, 1990, Table 7; HM Treasury, 1990, Tables 11.1 and 11.13)
Note: The university figure is for Great Britain

tion between regions in the amount spent per pupil, as indicated in Figure 8.10. Unit costs in metropolitan authorities have been consistently higher than in the shire counties. This is partly due to higher rates and premises costs and to the London weighting in salaries, and partly because of the extra demands placed on the education service by inner-city characteristics, such as high unemployment, widespread poverty and a greater diversity of cultures and languages. Urban Labour-controlled authorities have also been less likely to reduce their level of education spending in the face of public spending cuts, although their ability to avoid doing so has been diminished, first by rate-capping and now by charge-capping.

At the level of individual LEAs, differences in spending ranged from £1078 (Kent) to £1869 (ILEA) per primary school child in 1987–8, and from £1590 (Hereford and Worcester) to £2866 (ILEA) per secondary school pupil (CIPFA, 1989, pp. 17 and 49).

There are also regional variations in the proportion of the unit cost that is spent on different items, for example transport or books and equipment. Figure 8.11 shows that, apart from London, the different types of authority spend at a very similar level on books and equipment in special schools, but that in both primary and secondary schools, metropolitan districts spend on average less on books and equipment per child than the shire counties.

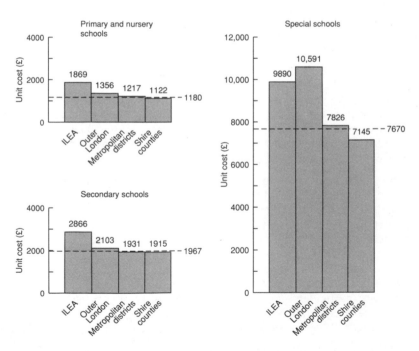

*Figure 8.10   Unit costs (per pupil per annum) of education, for different types of schools in different regions, England and Wales 1989–90
(Adapted from CIPFA, 1989)
Note: The ILEA was abolished from April 1990*

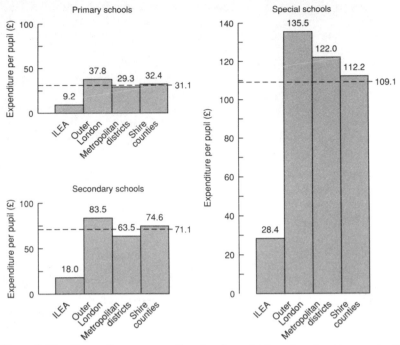

*Figure 8.11   Expenditure per pupil on books and educational equipment in different
regions, 1989–90 estimates
(Adapted from CIPFA, 1989)
Note: The ILEA was abolished from April 1990*

These figures mask large differences between individual LEAs: the high-
est-spending authorities spent almost five times as much as the lowest-
spending ones. (The ILEA figure cannot be taken at face value in its last,
incomplete, year. In previous years, it was consistently the highest spender
per capita on books and educational equipment.)

The pattern for spending on transport by different types of authority is
almost the reverse of that for books and equipment. The shire counties,
especially those in Wales, top the spending charts, with London and the
metropolitan districts at the bottom. LEAs in sparsely populated rural
areas have to pay the most for transport, the highest being £93 per primary
child and £175 per secondary child in Powys, Wales. The English
LEAs spending the most on transport were Norfolk for primary children
(£30) and Cornwall for secondary (£103). The differences between authorities are particularly marked in the case of special education. Transport
costs are much higher overall for this sector of education, but some LEAs
spent over £1000 on transport per pupil whereas others spent under £200.

Trends over time in unit costs   Unit costs for maintained schools have risen
in real terms throughout the 1980s — by 42% between 1979–80 and
1988–9. This is only partly explained by a fall in pupil numbers over the
same period of 17%. (If overall expenditure had remained the same in real

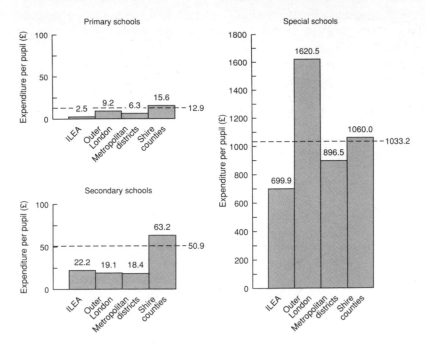

Figure 8.12   Expenditure per pupil on transport in different regions, 1989–90 estimates
(Adapted from CIPFA, 1989)
Note: The ILEA was abolished from April 1990

terms, a fall in pupil numbers of 17% would have led to a rise in unit costs of 20%) (HM Treasury, 1990, Table 11.10).

An increase in unit costs does not necessarily mean that a pupil gets proportionately more resources or better educational provision, as some costs are fixed (such as heating and cleaning) and they simply rise for each pupil as the school roll falls. In fact, spending per child on books and educational equipment increased slightly (though not steadily) in real terms during the 1980s in both primary and secondary schools. In 1989–90, spending on books and educational equipment was £31.40 in primary schools, and £60.90 in secondary (CIPFA, 1989). The comparable figures for 1978–9, adjusted to 1989–90 values, were £30.40 (primary) and £57.50 (secondary) (Weekly Hansard, 1986). Spending per child on books and equipment is much higher in secondary than in primary schools.

By contrast, unit costs in higher education have fallen in real terms during the 1980s — by 37% in universities and 21% in polytechnics and colleges (HM Treasury, 1990, Table 11.16).

Pupil/teacher ratio and class size
Another measure of the resources available in education is the pupil/teacher ratio (PTR), calculated by dividing the number of pupils by the number of qualified teachers or full-time teacher equivalents. It is lower in

private than in maintained schools (i.e. there are fewer pupils per teacher), and it is lowest of all in special schools. As schools rolls have declined, so the PTR has fallen.

Although the PTR is the measure on which decisions about resource allocation are often based, it is the size of the class as taught which has greater implications for children's learning experience. Class sizes are generally larger than PTRs, because not all teachers actually teach (heads, for instance, spend most of their time on administrative work), because marking and preparation duties restrict direct contact hours with pupils, and because sometimes classes are combined or split up for various periods.

Changes over time, and variations between different countries of the United Kingdom in PTRs are illustrated in Chapter 5 (see especially Figures 5.8 and 5.12). There is also variation between LEAs. For example, the PTR in English and Welsh primary schools in 1989–90 varied from 17.4 to 1 in the ILEA to over 23 to 1 in Cheshire, Clwyd and Hereford and Worcester. And the PTR in English secondary schools in 1987 varied from 12 to 1 in the London Borough of Waltham Forest to over 16 to 1 in Bedfordshire, Essex, Suffolk and the Isle of Wight. (The very lowest PTR of any English LEA was in the Isles of Scilly, but it had under 300 pupils in total) (CIPFA, 1989).

School meals and milk

In 1980, responsibility for the provision of school meals passed from central government to the LEAs. They were initially required to provide free meals for children in families receiving Supplementary Benefit, and to provide a place for children to eat food they brought from home, but otherwise the level, type and price of provision, if any, was left to the discretion of the individual LEA. By 1986, however, all obligations on LEAs to provide meals were removed, and their powers to supply free meals reduced. (See Chapter 4: 1980 Education Act; 1986 Social Security Act.) Most authorities now operate a cafeteria system in secondary schools, although a fixed-price system is still more common in primary schools. The average cost of a primary school fixed-price meal in 1986 was 61p, although some authorities such as the ILEA provided heavy subsidies to make this figure much lower.

About half of the pupils in maintained schools take school meals, with the rest bringing their own food or making other arrangements (mostly going home for lunch). In 1986, some authorities provided no canteen facilities at all (e.g. Buckinghamshire), while in other authorities a substantial proportion of children took paid school meals (e.g. Derbyshire, with 56%). There is also considerable variation in the proportion of pupils receiving free school meals. The average in England and Wales in 1989–90 was 11%, but this figure masks variations, from 26% in the ILEA to 6% in the Outer London boroughs. Some of the variation is due to differences in LEA policies and some to socioeconomic variation between the local populations. Figure 8.13 shows the national averages for various ways of taking meals at school.

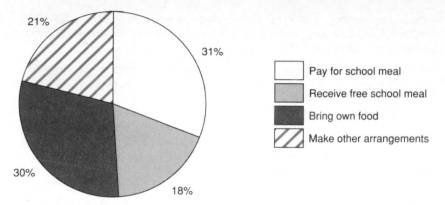

21%

31%

30%

18%

☐ Pay for school meal

▨ Receive free school meal

■ Bring own food

⧄ Make other arrangements

Figure 8.13 Types of meals at school, maintained schools, England, October 1986 (Adapted from CIPFA, 1986)

Scotland

Expenditure on education in Scotland, apart from universities, is the responsibility, directly or indirectly (through influence on local authorities) of the Secretary of State for Scotland. Together with such services as health, roads and transport, law and order and housing, it falls within a category of spending programmes known as the Scottish Block. The Block comprised nearly 96% of all expenditure within the Secretary of State's responsibility in 1989–90. (The remaining 4%, though formally within his responsibility too, was in practice for programmes determined by United Kingdom or European Community policies.) The total Scottish Block is calculated each year by simply adopting the changes in expenditure agreed for comparable programmes in England and Wales, adjusted for the differences in population.

The Secretary of State then decides how to distribute this total among individual services. In 1989–90, total expenditure in the Scottish Block was an estimated £8.6 billion. Of this, £309 million was allocated to the central government's (i.e. the Scottish Office's) own direct expenditure on education, and a further £5 million earmarked for the various education authorities (i.e. the Regional and Islands Councils) to spend on education. But this sum — under 4% of the Block — represents only a small fraction of spending from the Block on education in Scotland. Much more money comes from it to education in the shape of the funds allocated by the Secretary of State to local authorities through the Revenue Support Grant: £2.3 billion in 1989–90. The local authorities decide how to distribute this grant among the various services they provide — together with the money they themselves raise from Community Charge — but the Secretary of State each year indicates in advance what he thinks their 'Total Standard Spending', and their 'Standard Spending' on each service ought to be. The authorities need not follow his recommendations, but like his counterparts in England and Wales, he has powers to cap their Community Charge levels if he judges that they are overspending. For 1990–1, the Total Standard Spending has been set at £4.9 billion, of which the Standard Spending on education is £2.2 billion (45%).

The actual spending on education and other major services in 1989–90 — by the Scottish Office and local authorities combined — is shown in Figure 8.14. Only Health was a bigger spender than education; other services had much less money spent on them. (The spending of the Department of Social Security and the Ministry of Defence is not included here.) Most of the educational expenditure (86% — £2.2 billion) was local authority current expenditure, and most of that (about two-thirds) was for wages and salaries. An additional 3% was local authority capital expenditure. The remaining 11% of the total educational expenditure in 1989–90 was direct spending by the Scottish Office, mostly on higher education: student awards and grants to Colleges of Education and Central Institutions. It did not include any grants to the universities in Scotland, which are the responsibility of the DES (HM Treasury, 1990, Tables 15.1, 15.2 and 21.4.12).

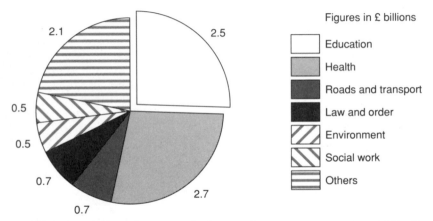

Figures in £ billions

☐ Education

▨ Health

▨ Roads and transport

■ Law and order

▨ Environment

▨ Social work

☰ Others

Figure 8.14   Estimated Scottish Block expenditure on major services, 1989–90 (Adapted from HM Treasury, 1990, Tables 13.1 and 15.2)

Northern Ireland

As with Scottish public expenditure, the total 'Northern Ireland Block' and its division between services are announced in the government's annual white paper. In 1989–90, the estimated expenditure of the major services was as shown in Figure 8.15. As in the rest of the United Kingdom, education is one of the highest spenders; only Health spends more.

Unlike those in the rest of the United Kingdom, Northern Ireland's local educational authorities, the Education and Library Boards, receive all their funding from central government, here the Department of Education Northern Ireland (DENI). The percentages of the total expenditure of the

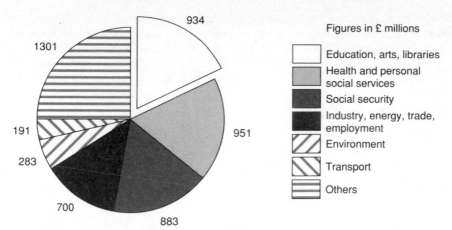

Figures in £ millions

☐ Education, arts, libraries
▨ Health and personal social services
■ Social security
■ Industry, energy, trade, employment
▨ Environment
▨ Transport
▤ Others

Figure 8.15   Estimated expenditure by major departments, Northern Ireland 1989–90
(Adapted from HM Treasury, 1990, Tables 17.1 and 17.2)
Note: Expenditure excludes that of the Army in Northern Ireland

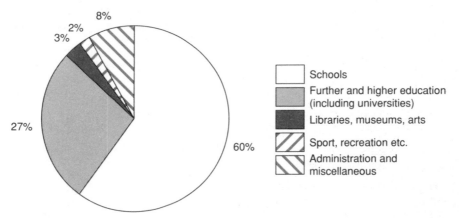

☐ Schools
▨ Further and higher education (including universities)
■ Libraries, museums, arts
▨ Sport, recreation etc.
▨ Administration and miscellaneous

Figure 8.16   Planned allocation of expenditure by DENI and Education and Library Boards to main groups of services, 1990–1
(Adapted from HM Treasury, 1990, Table 17.13)

DENI and boards allocated to their five main groups of services are shown in Figure 8.16.

Sources and further reading

Two principal sources of information on educational finance are especially helpful. First are the publications of the Chartered Institute of Public Finance and Accountancy (CIPFA), especially (for 'Where the money comes from') its *Financial Information Services*, Volumes 18 (*Resources*) and 20 (*Education*); these are published in loose-leaf form and usually kept up to date section by section as required, though as we go to press (late

1990), they have not yet caught up with the recent changes. Second (mainly for 'Where the money goes') is the latest of the government's annual white papers on public expenditure (HM Treasury, 1990). For the financial consequences of the 1988 Education Reform Act, Maclure (1989) is again invaluable; see Chapters 3 and 6. These and other useful sources are listed below.

CIPFA (1986) *School Meals Statistics, October 1986*, London, Chartered Institute of Public Finance and Accountancy.

CIPFA (1989) *Education Statistics: 1989/90 Estimates*, London, Chartered Institute of Public Finance and Accountancy.

CIPFA (1990) *Handbook of Education Unit Costs 1987/88*, London, Chartered Institute of Public Finance and Accountancy.

CIPFA (no single date — a) *Financial Information Services*, Vol. 18, *Resources*, London, Chartered Institute of Public Finance and Accountancy.

CIPFA (no single date — b) *Financial Information Services*, Vol. 20, *Education*, London, Chartered Institute of Public Finance and Accountancy.

DES (1987) *Statistical Bulletin 14/87: Education Expenditure 1981–82 to 1985–86*, London, Department of Education and Science.

DES (1988) *Statistical Bulletin 2/88: Pupil/Teacher Ratios for each Local Education Authority in England, January 1987*, London, Department of Education and Science.

DES (1989) *Statistical Bulletin 1/89: Education Statistics for the United Kingdom 1988 edition*, London, Department of Education and Science.

HM Treasury (1990) *The Government's Expenditure Plans 1990–91 to 1992–93*, London, HMSO.

Lightfoot, L. (1990) 'Scandal of our schools', *The Mail on Sunday*, 27 May 1990, pp. 1–2.

Maclure, S. (1989) *Education Re-Formed: a guide to the Education Reform Act*, 2nd edn, London, Hodder & Stoughton.

Sumner, R. and Hutchinson, D. (1990) *Resources in Primary Schools*, Slough, National Foundation for Educational Research.

Weekly Hansard (1986) *House of Commons Parliamentary Debates*, Vol. 97, Column 44: Written Answers, 6 May 1986, London, HMSO.

CHAPTER 9 EXAMINATIONS AND QUALIFICATIONS

Qualifications are of many different kinds and levels. Some are predominantly academic, others vocational. Some are normally obtained through study at school, others through further education. Courses leading to qualifications up to and including A level or its equivalent are generally referred to as *non-advanced further education* (NAFE); qualifications above A-level standard as *advanced further education* (AFE).

Many are undergoing considerable change at present. In schools, O level and CSE have been replaced by GCSE in England, Wales and Northern Ireland; and O grade has been replaced by Standard grade in Scotland. In vocational and 'pre-vocational' training, there are at present very large numbers of different qualifications (and of awarding bodies), not always widely recognised or even understood; but simpler structures are currently emerging.

School and non-advanced further education: academic

CSE (Certificate of Secondary Education)
Introduced in 1965, the CSE was replaced in 1988 by the GCSE. It was aimed at the top 60% of school pupils, and was usually taken by 15- and 16-year-olds. There were three types ('modes'), depending on whether the syllabus and/or examination were set by an examining board or a school.

GCE O level (General Certificate of Education)
Introduced in 1951, the GCE O level was also replaced in 1988 by the GCSE. It was aimed at the top 20% of school pupils, and again was usually taken by 15- and 16-year-olds. Until 1975, each examining board awarded its own grades, usually 1 to 9, with 1 to 6 being passes. After 1975, the grades were changed to A to E, with, in theory, no fail grades. However, the C/D boundary was defined as equivalent to the old pass/fail boundary and, in practice, A to C are still widely regarded as pass grades, D and E as fail.

SCE O grade (Scottish Certificate of Education)
This was the Scottish equivalent of the GCE O level and was introduced in 1962 for the top 30% of school pupils. From 1986 it was replaced by Standard grade.

GCSE (General Certificate of Secondary Education)
In 1986, GCSE courses were introduced to replace both CSE and GCE O levels, creating a single examination system in England, Wales and Northern Ireland for those aged 16 or over (though younger pupils can be entered). GCSE is awarded on a 7-point scale, with much emphasis placed on course work as well as a final examination. The first examinations took place in summer 1988.

SCE Standard grade

In 1984, the first SCE Standard grade courses started to replace O grades in Scotland, with the first examinations in 1986. They are to be taken by all pupils, but with three levels of study and award (Foundation, General and Credit). Pupils receive a certificate at the end of their fourth year giving a 'profile' of their abilities (see Chapter 3, 1977 Dunning).

GCE A level

Introduced in 1951 in England, Wales and Northern Ireland, A levels are aimed at the most academically able pupils. About 10% of school pupils take two or more A levels, usually in full-time education in school or FE college, between the ages of 17 and 19. They are widely used as entrance qualifications for higher education. In 1988, the Higginson Report recommended that A levels should cover a wide range of subjects, with candidates normally taking five A levels rather than two or three. However, the government's immediate response was to reject this proposal.

SCE Higher grade

The SCE Higher is the Scottish alternative to the A level. Unlike A levels, Highers are taken one year after O grade rather than two, and over four or five subjects rather than two or three. As a rough guide, four Highers are regarded as equivalent to two A levels.

AS level (Advanced Supplementary)

This is a new examination to be taken alongside A levels, involving about half the work of an A level, and aimed at broadening the curriculum. It has been available since September 1987, with the first examinations in summer 1989.

CSYS (Certificate of Sixth Year Studies)

The CSYS is a qualification available to Scottish 18-year-olds after a year of study following Highers, which are taken at 17.

CEE (Certificate of Extended Education)

In 1973, the CEE was introduced as an experiment to meet the needs of the 'new sixth', that is, 17-year-olds who, under the comprehensive system, wanted to stay on at school for another year but not to take A levels. Though never officially endorsed by the Secretary of State, it has proved popular and several examining boards have resisted pressure to drop it in favour of CPVE. (See below: Joint Board for Pre-vocational Education; see also Chapter 3, 1979 Keohane.)

School and non-advanced further education: pre-vocational and vocational

There are, at present, about 6000 pre-vocational and vocational qualifications in all, awarded by about 6000 different qualifying bodies (Rogers, 1988, p. 26). In England, Wales and Northern Ireland, the government, while unifying some of these (see below: Business and Technician Education Council; Joint Board for Pre-vocational Education), plans to preserve much of the existing range and variety of qualifications, though setting them in a more coherent and intelligible framework (see below: National Council for Vocational Qualifications). In Scotland, however, all non-advanced FE courses are now to be directed towards a single qualification (see below: Scottish Vocational Education Council).

The main bodies awarding qualifications in England and Wales, established and new, with some of their principal qualifications, include the following.

Royal Society of Arts (RSA)
The RSA is an established body, offering a range of qualifications for office and commercial work and languages. These can be taken on a full- or part-time basis, usually in FE colleges, but also in some schools. There are three stages of award: Elementary, Intermediate and Advanced. (The RSA Pre-vocational Course, offering a basic qualification in secretarial and clerical skills, is intended to be replaced by CPVE; see below: Joint Board for Pre-vocational Education.)

London Chamber of Commerce and Industry (LCCI)
This is an established body, offering a variety of qualifications in business, secretarial and language studies, again at three levels (Elementary, Intermediate and Higher).

City and Guilds of London Institute (CGLI)
This established body provides training for most of the craft industries, offering over 200 subjects from hairdressing to engineering. Many job advertisements specify the precise City and Guilds Certificate required by number, e.g. CGLI 599 in construction services welding or CGLI 465 in tailoring. Three tiers of certificate are offered: Part 1, usually taken after one or two years part-time study; Part 2 or Final Certificate after another two years; and a Part 3 or Advanced Certificate is available in some subjects, usually including some training for management. The CGLI has also developed special schemes for YTS trainees. It is an independent body and the courses are drawn up by specialist committees including representatives from government, industry and teaching. From 1988, candidates will be able to take CGLI examinations on a modular basis, building up credits rather than having to sit the examination for the full certificate at one time. (The CGLI Foundation Course, aimed at those aged 16 or over and offering general education linked to a specific area of work, and the CGLI Vocational Preparation (General) Course, allowing students unsure of their plans to try various general areas of work, are both intended to be replaced by CPVE; see below: Joint Board for Pre-vocational Education.)

Business and Technician Education Council (BTEC)
Formed in 1983 by an amalgamation of the Business Education Council and the Technician Education Council, the BTEC offers training for jobs in industry, commerce and administration. Each of the three levels of training (First, National and Higher National) can be taken as a Certificate (usually two years part-time alongside employment) or as a Diploma (normally two years full-time or three years sandwich). The National

qualifications are a vocational equivalent to academic A levels, the Higher National to ordinary degrees. These qualifications replace the Ordinary and Higher National Certificates and Diplomas (ONC/OND, HNC/HND) that preceded them. (The BTEC General Award, a general business studies qualification for those aged 16 or over with few previous formal qualifications, is being replaced by CPVE; see below: Joint Board for Pre-vocational Education.)

Joint Board for Pre-vocational Education

This new board has been set up with equal representation from CGLI and BTEC to validate and examine courses for the Certificate of Pre-vocational Education (CPVE). This is a qualification available to school sixth formers and FE college students from autumn 1986 (sometimes referred to as the '17 plus'). It consists of a certificate plus a 'profile' of individual abilities and achievements, following a year of full-time study. Courses are intended to prepare the student for adult life and work generally, not for particular jobs. They are designed by individual schools or colleges but have to follow a formal framework of core studies, vocational options and 'additional' elements, and are subject to approval by the joint board. The CPVE is intended to replace some of the existing qualifications of the CGLI, BTEC and other bodies (see above).

National Council for Vocational Qualifications (NCVQ)

The NCVQ is not an examining body in its own right but was established, in 1986, to monitor existing awarding bodies and their qualifications in England, Wales and Northern Ireland — approving those that meet certain standards, which it will set, and showing where they stand in relation to one another. By 1991, those it approves are to be designated National Vocational Qualifications (NVQ), and accorded one of four levels: Basic, Standard, Advanced and Higher.

Scottish Vocational Education Council (SCOTVEC)

Since 1984, the SCOTVEC has offered a National Certificate, to which all non-advanced FE courses in Scotland are to be directed. National Certificate courses are modular in structure, with students receiving credits for units of up to 40 hours' study. They are designed to be equivalent in standard to existing qualifications, such as those of the RSA and CGLI, and to replace them in Scotland. National Certificate courses can be taken in FE colleges, central institutions or secondary schools, and students can transfer between these institutions, or between them and other forms of training. The National Certificate is also to cover technical and craft training, and the 'off-the-job' component of training schemes like YTS. Students can follow National Certificate courses alongside other courses (such as Highers).

Advanced further education

Diploma in Higher Education (DipHE)

The DipHE is a qualification, validated by the CNAA or a university, that is gained after two years of study in a college of higher education. A qualification in its own right, it is, however, often now extended by further study to a degree. It was first introduced in 1974.

Professional awards
These are specialised qualifications necessary for working in particular professions, such as architecture, law and accountancy; they are awarded by the professional body concerned. (Relevant BTEC diplomas and certificates sometimes count towards exemptions.)

Degree
Degrees are awarded by universities, polytechnics, colleges and institutes of higher education, and some FE colleges. Universities have the right to award their own degrees; polytechnic and college degrees have to be validated (that is, approved and underwritten), usually by the Council for National Academic Awards (CNAA) but occasionally by a university. In 1986, about two-thirds of degree students were studying for university degrees and one third for CNAA degrees. Normally a degree at a university (apart from the Open University) requires three or four years' full-time study, but it may be taken as a four-year sandwich course, or in five to six years' part-time study in other institutions. At the Open University, degree studies are part-time, and mainly by correspondence.

Degrees may be 'first degrees' or 'higher degrees' (see below). Most first degrees carry the title 'bachelor': Bachelor of Arts (BA), Bachelor of Science (BSc), Bachelor of Education (BEd), Bachelor of Engineering (BEng) and so on. At the four ancient Scottish universities, however, first degrees in art faculties are generally called Master of Arts (MA), although the newer Scottish universities and the CNAA in Scotland follow the English system and award bachelor degrees. Labels such as 'arts' or 'science' do not necessarily indicate the content of a course; some institutions award a BA in almost every discipline, including science and engineering.

First degrees are normally awarded at honours and ordinary (or pass) levels, with honours degrees further divided into first class, second class (upper and lower) and third class.

PGCE (Postgraduate Certificate of Education)
This is a one-year teacher-training qualification for those who already have a first degree. It is offered by universities, polytechnics and other colleges of higher education.

Higher degree
Higher degrees are available to those who already hold a first degree (especially a first-class or upper-second-class honours). Higher degrees are of two basic kinds — taught degrees (for which one normally sits an examination) and research degrees (for which one normally submits a thesis) — and of three basic levels.

The lowest level — usually, but not always, called 'masters' degrees — may be by either teaching or research, and may require one or two years of full-time study (or the equivalent in part-time study). There is no uniformity of terminology between institutions: such degrees include MA, MSc,

MEd, MBA, MPhil, MLitt, etc. However, the word 'master' does not always appear in the name of a postgraduate degree: BPhil, BLitt, LlB, BD and even sometimes BSc can be postgraduate degrees. Nor are all 'masters' degrees postgraduate: the four ancient Scottish universities call their undergraduate arts degree an MA. Furthermore, a masters degree may not even be a qualification in the usual sense at all: Oxford and Cambridge University BA graduates can, after a specified number of years, obtain an MA without any further study or assessment.

The next level — called 'Doctor of Philosophy' (PhD or occasionally DPhil) regardless of the subject of study – is a more advanced qualification requiring the submission of a thesis based on original research, and usually assumed to take three years of full-time study.

Finally, 'higher doctorates' (such as DSc, DLitt, DD) are awarded for distinguished contribution to an academic field, actually on the basis of books or other publications over a period of years.

Honorary degree
Awarded by universities according to any criteria they wish, honorary degrees are usually given as a mark of respect, congratulation or gratitude. They do not necessarily reflect or indicate any academic achievement. They normally take the form of higher degrees, occasionally masters degrees but more usually higher doctorates (Hon. DSc, Hon. LlD, etc.); holders of honorary doctorates do not normally adopt the title 'Doctor'.

Sources and further reading

CRAC (1987) *Directory of Further Education 1987/88*, London, Careers Research and Advisory Centre.

DES (1985) *Education and Training for Young People: A White Paper*, London, HMSO.

DES (1985) *Annual Report 1985*, London, Department of Education and Science.

DES (1987) *NAFE in Practice: An HMI Survey*, London, HMSO.

O'Connor, M. (1986) *A Parents' Guide to Education*, London, Fontana.

Rogers, R. (1988) A is for acronym, *School Governor*, No. 2, March 1988.

CHAPTER 10 CURRICULUM AND ITS ASSESSMENT

England and Wales

One of the most dramatic innovations of the 1988 Education Reform Act is the introduction of a compulsory curriculum, together with elaborate arrangements for assessing how it is being taught and learnt.

For more than 40 years, since the passage of the 1944 Education Act, central government had no formal role in determining the curriculum of schools; it probably had little role in practice for several years before. The 1944 Act specified only one compulsory subject for schools — religious education — and even there individual pupils could opt out if their parents wished. Otherwise, the design of the curriculum was left formally to local education authorities, and in practice largely to head teachers — in association with governors after the 1986 Education Act (see Chapter 4).

In reality, of course, the structure and contents of school curricula were subject to many constraints. These included such interrelated factors as GCE examination boards, university entrance requirements, HMI visits and reports, and the demands of parents. There was no single set pattern of subjects, but it would have been difficult for a school to neglect totally those regarded as basic and normal. Shortly before the introduction of the national curriculum, the percentages of time actually spent by the average secondary fourth and fifth year child in England on what were to become the national curriculum subjects (see below) of the 1988 Act, or their nearest equivalents, were as shown in Figure 10.1.

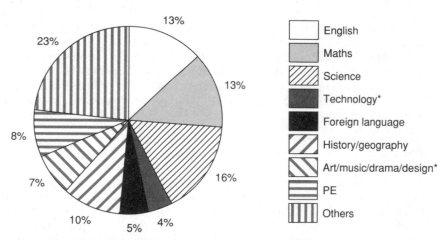

Figure 10.1   Percentage of time devoted to national curriculum subjects by fourth- and fifth-year pupils, England 1984
(Adapted from DES, 1987, Table 5)
Note: The national curriculum categories of 'Technology' and 'Design' were not used in the DES 1984 survey; the figures for 'Craft-based CDT' and 'Design-based CDT' respectively have been used here in their place

Structure of the national curriculum

The 1988 Education Reform Act, however, prescribes a compulsory curriculum for all maintained schools in England and Wales. Like the 1944 Act, it makes religious education compulsory, together with religious worship that will normally be 'broadly Christian' in character. In addition, it prescribes a *national curriculum*, consisting of up to eleven *foundation subjects*, three or four of which are to form a *core*.

The core subjects are *mathematics*, *English* and *science* — these apply to all ages and all parts of the country. In addition, *Welsh* is a core subject in schools in Wales that are Welsh-speaking.

The other foundation subjects are *history*, *geography*, *technology*, *music*, *art* and *physical education* — again these apply to all ages and all parts of the country. In addition, *Welsh* is a foundation subject in schools in Wales that are not Welsh-speaking. And a *modern foreign language*, as approved by the Secretary of State, is a foundation subject at secondary, but not primary level.

The Act also empowers the Secretary of State to define the structure and content of each of these subjects in considerable detail, and to specify what pupils of different abilities should study and achieve at various ages. Four *key stages* in a child's education are defined, ending at the ages of 7, 11, 14 and 16. For each key stage, *programmes of study* are to be drawn up specifying what pupils of different abilities are to be taught in each subject, and *attainment targets* set out specifying the knowledge, skills and understanding that they are expected to have acquired by the end of the stage. Finally, *assessment arrangements* are to be made, to test pupils' actual attainments at the end of each stage in relation to the attainment targets set.

Thus, the Act itself establishes only a skeleton structure for the national curriculum and its assessment, empowering the Secretary of State to decide most of the substance in subsequent Orders. To advise him or her in these decisions, the Act establishes three statutory bodies, the National Curriculum Council (for England), the Curriculum Council for Wales, and the School Examinations and Assessment Council. The members of these Councils are nominated by the Secretary of State. Before issuing an Order under the Act, he or she must consult the appropriate council, and though not obliged to take their advice, is obliged to publish it, and to give reasons if it is rejected.

The implementation of the national curriculum is planned to take place progressively during the years of 1989–90 to 1996–7. The Secretary of State began the process by setting up working groups to make recommendations for the three core subjects of mathematics, English and science (and technology, the first of the other foundation subjects). The working groups produced their reports in 1989, and on the basis of them, the Secretary of State drew up and published programmes of study and attainment targets in all four subjects. The actual teaching of the national curriculum could then begin.

It is still uncertain how much time schools will have to devote to the national curriculum and its various subjects, and how much they will be able to give to other activities. In a consultation document issued before the publication of the Education Reform Bill that subsequently became the 1988 Act, the Secretaries of State for Education and Science and for Wales gave one example of how the national curriculum might be divided in practice. In the fourth and fifth years of secondary education, they suggested, the foundation subjects might account for some 75–85% of pupils' time (30–40% of that devoted to the core subjects), leaving some 15–25% of time for other subjects, at the discretion of the school (DES/Welsh Office, 1987). This is illustrated in Figure 10.2. No more detailed official guidance has been given in the succeeding years.

(If we compare this figure with Figure 10.1, we must remember that the picture before 1988 was an *average* of more or less varied individual curricula, whereas the picture after 1988 is, at least in its general outlines, the same for *every* child.)

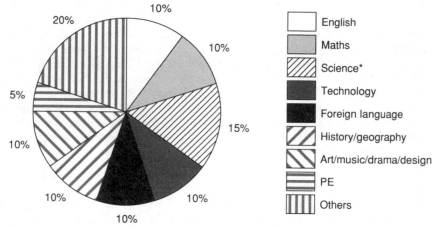

Figure 10.2   The national curriculum for fourth and fifth years of secondary schools: an example
(Adapted from DES/Welsh Office, 1987)
Note: The allocation for 'Combined sciences' in the DES/Welsh Office example is 10–20% of curriculum time. In the figure, this is shown as 15%

Introducing the national curriculum

The national curriculum began to be taught in the autumn of 1989, with pupils in the first year of Key Stage 1 introduced to the programmes of study and attainment targets of the three core subjects of mathematics, English and science. In addition, pupils in the first year of Key Stage 3 were to be introduced by the summer of 1990 to the programmes of study and attainment targets in two of these subjects: mathematics and science.

During the school year 1990–1, further developments are to take place: pupils at a new Key Stage (2) are to be introduced to the three core subjects; a new subject (design and technology) is to be introduced to pupils in the first three key stages; and for the first time, pupils (at Key Stage 1) are to face assessment. And so it is planned to continue, year by year, until the entire national curriculum is in place by the end of 1997. (The official timetable for its implementation is reprinted in a number of places, e.g. Maclure, 1989, pp. 24–5.)

Assessing the national curriculum

In addition to the subject working groups, the Secretary of State set up a Task Group on Testing and Assessment (TGAT), which reported in early 1988 with recommendations for assessment arrangements for the national curriculum; by and large, these were accepted by the Secretary of State. As yet, it is possible only to outline in general terms how the arrangements will work. Full details will become known as the successive subject working groups report, and programmes of study and attainment targets are drawn up.

In general, then, children are to be assessed at the end of each of the key stages (i.e. at 7, 11, 14 and 16); at the first stage, the assessment will be in the three core subjects, but at subsequent stages, it will be in all the foundation subjects. At each stage, the children will be assessed against appropriate attainment targets, which are to be grouped for the purpose into a small number (the Task Group recommended no more than four) of *profile components*, which will reflect the range of knowledge, skills and understanding the subject encompasses. For each profile component, there is to be a progression through ten *levels* of achievement — the same scale of levels to be used to assess children at every stage. So, all children can be compared in their attainments directly with one another, regardless of age. And as the years pass, it is argued, children will be aware of making progress. Rather than tending to achieve constantly a similar grade or mark (whether a low of a high one) on tests with ever higher standards, they will constantly be increasing their own level of attainment on the same scale of levels.

The assessment is to be of two basic forms, first the teachers' own judgements of their pupils, based on their work in class, and secondly, the pupils' performances on *standard assessment tasks* (SATs). Procedures for monitoring the teachers' assessments are to be established — especially where there is disagreement between the results of the two forms. At the final key stage (age 16), assessment is likely to be mainly through the GCSE.

As well as results for individual children, which will be made available to their parents, there will be compulsory publication of aggregated test results — by class, by school and by LEA — for Key Stages 2, 3 and 4. This is the most controversial part of the assessment arrangements. The government's declared aim is to enable parents to judge how well teachers, schools and LEAs are performing, a judgement of increased significance after the 1988 Act, with open enrolment, and schools' budgets heavily dependent on their pupil numbers. But critics argue that comparisons between schools based on differences in aggregated test results will often be unfair and misleading, since these results depend in large part on factors outside the control of schools, notably the social characteristics of the community from which the children are drawn.

Scotland

The 1988 Education Act does not apply to Scotland, which has no statutory curriculum. However, in 1977 the Munn Report recommended a common curriculum for the third and fourth years of Scottish secondary schools. This was a complicated structure of a two-tier core plus an elective area (see Chapter 3 for details), and it is uncertain how much effect it has had on the actual practice of schools. The percentages of pupils' time recommended by Munn for the various subjects are shown in Figure 10.3.

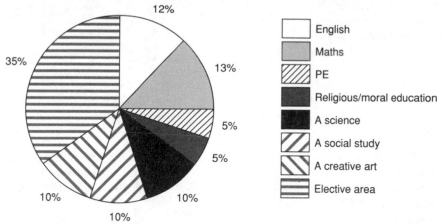

Figure 10.3   *Percentage of time recommended for core and elective areas of the Scottish secondary curriculum*
(Adapted from Scottish Education Department, 1977)

Northern Ireland

Northern Ireland is introducing comparable reforms to those in England and Wales (DENI, 1989; see Chapter 4 above). These include the introduction of a *Northern Ireland curriculum* for all children of compulsory school age in grant-aided schools, and a pattern of assessment criteria and attainment testing much as in England and Wales (though the first key stage is to end at the age of 8, not 7, and Irish is to be a foundation subject in Irish-speaking schools). A Northern Ireland Curriculum Council and School Examinations and Assessment Council have been established to advise the DENI and supervise the preparation of programmes of study and assessment criteria.

Unlike England and Wales, however, Northern Ireland has retained a selective (rather than a comprehensive) system of secondary education, which gives particular significance to the proposed attainment tests at 11. The government favours using these new tests as a replacement for the current methods of testing at that age for admission to grammar secondary schools (which emphasise verbal reasoning rather than attainment).

Attitudes to the curriculum

Just before the publication of the Bill that became the 1988 Education Reform Act, opinion in Great Britain was evenly divided over whether control of the curriculum should be in the hands of local education authorities or of central government; this is shown in Figure 10.4.

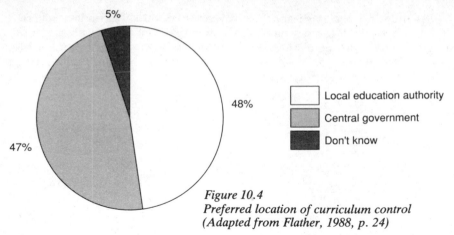

Figure 10.4
Preferred location of curriculum control
(Adapted from Flather, 1988, p. 24)

These attitudes vary sharply by political allegiance: over 60% of Conservative Party supporters thought control should be in the hands of central government, and over 60% of Labour Party supporters thought control should rest with LEAs.

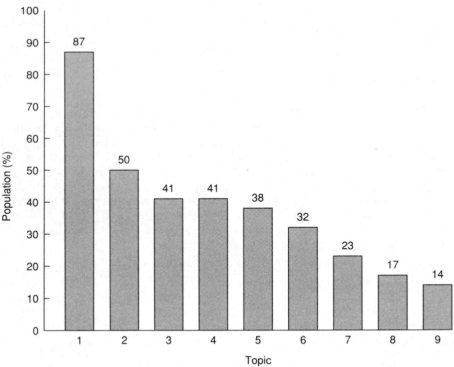

Figure 10.5   Percentage of population considering specific curriculum topics essential for 15-year-olds
(Adapted from Goldstein, 1986, Table 6.9)
Note: Key to topics: 1 Reading, writing and mathematics; 2 Discipline and orderliness; 3 Respect for authority; 4 Ability to make one's own judgements; 5 Job training; 6 Science and technology; 7 Concern for minorities and the poor; 8 Sex education; 9 History, literature and the arts

Attitudes in Great Britain before the publication of the Bill to the content of the curriculum are illustrated in Figure 10.5, which shows the percentages of respondents who considered particular topics to be essential for 15 year olds.

There is little variation by sex or social class in these attitudes, and little consistent variation with age except that the older the respondents, the more likely they are to consider *Respect for authority* and *Discipline and orderliness* essential, and the less likely to consider *Sex education* essential.

Sources and further reading

DES (1987) *Statistical Bulletin 10/87: The 1984 Secondary School Staffing Survey — Data on the curriculum in maintained secondary schools in England*, London, Department of Education and Science.

DES/Welsh Office (1987) *The National Curriculum 5–16: a consultation document*, London/Cardiff.

DENI (1989) *The Education Reform (Northern Ireland) Order 1989*, Belfast, HMSO.

Flather, P. (1988) Education Matters, in Jowell, R., Witherspoon, S. and Brooks, L. (eds) *British Social Attitudes: the 5th report*, Aldershot, Gower Publishing.

Goldstein, H. (1986) Interim Report: Education, in Jowell, R., Witherspoon, S. and Brooks, L. (eds) *British Social Attitudes: the 1986 report*, Aldershot, Gower Publishing.

Scottish Education Department (1977) *The Structure of the Curriculum in the Third and Fourth Years of Scottish Secondary Education* ('The Munn Report'), Edinburgh, HMSO.

CHAPTER 11 ACHIEVEMENT AND INEQUALITY

As measured by examination performance, educational achievement in secondary schools in the United Kingdom has increased during the 1970s and 1980s (especially in the 1970s). The increase has been slight at A level, but considerable at O level and CSE, as Figure 11.1 shows. A much smaller percentage of pupils now leaves school without any qualifications.

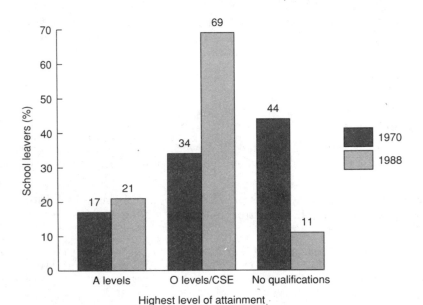

Figure 11.1   Highest level of attainment of school leavers in the United Kingdom, 1970 and 1988
(Adapted from Government Statistical Service, 1989, Table 31)
Note: For Scotland, Highers are counted in place of A levels, and O grades or Standard grades in place of O levels

There is some variation in educational achievement from country to country within the United Kingdom. Most notably, a higher percentage of school leavers achieves one or more A level passes in Northern Ireland (24.0%) than in England and Wales (18.7%); but at the same time, a higher percentage of pupils leaves school with *no* GCE or CSE qualifications in Northern Ireland (20.0%) than in England and Wales (9.9%). (The Scottish figures are not directly comparable.) (Government Statistical Service, 1989, Table 31.)

During the 1980s, there has been a slight increase in the percentages of young people over 16 staying on at school, as Figure 11.2 shows (see also Chapter 5, Figure 5.19 and Chapter 12, Figure 12.5).

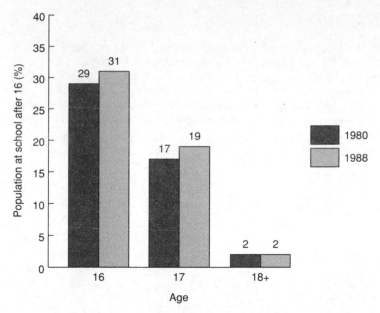

Figure 11.2   Percentage of population staying on at school after 16, 1980 and 1988 (Adapted from Government Statistical Service, 1982, Table 29, and 1989, Table 21)

Educational achievement as measured by participation in higher education has also increased during the past decade, as Figure 11.3 shows.

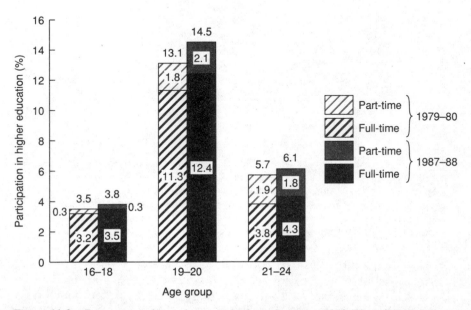

Figure 11.3   Percentage of population in higher education, 1979–80 and 1987–8 (Adapted from Government Statistical Service, 1982, Table 29, and 1989, Table 22)

Inequality

Education in the United Kingdom is characterised by numerous inequalities in achievement and provision, not only between individuals but also between social groups and categories. The rest of this chapter provides data about three different dimensions of inequality: sex, ethnic group and social class; it also gives some information about educational achievement in independent schools, and about the education of children with special needs.

Sex

Differences between the sexes in educational participation and achievement are much better documented than any other dimensions of inequality. This is because sex is one of the principal categories used in the collection and publication of official statistics on education. The measures of educational achievement discussed above all show differences between the sexes. Figure 11.4 shows how girls do better, overall, than boys in school examinations at all levels.

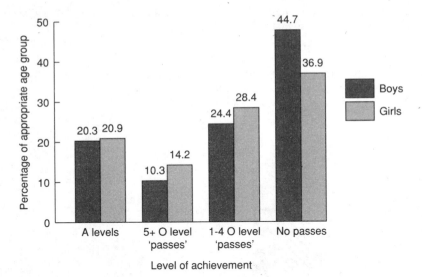

Figure 11.4   School leavers with different levels of achievement as percentage of appropriate age group of each sex, United Kingdom 1987–8
(Adapted from Government Statistical Service, 1989, Table 31)
Note: SCE H, O or Standard grades are taken as equivalent to GCE A and O levels respectively; 'passes' are GCE O level (SCE O or Standard grade) A–C or CSE grade 1; 'no passes' are lower grades or no graded results

However, sex differences in achievement are not uniformly in favour of girls across all subjects: while girls regularly achieve higher numbers of passes in some subjects, boys consistently achieve higher numbers in others. Figures 11.5 and 11.6 illustrate this for England, showing the number of 'passes' by boys and by girls in some of the most popular

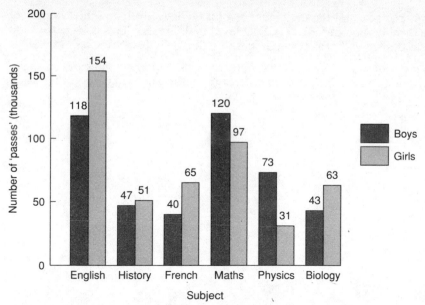

Figure 11.5   GCSE/O level/CSE 'passes', England 1988
(Adapted from DES, 1988, Table C12)
Note to Figures 11.5–11.7: A 'pass' is here taken at GCSE and O level to be grades
A–C, and at CSE to be grade 1

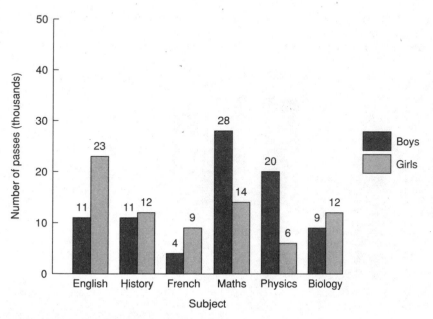

Figure 11.6   A level passes, England 1988
(Adapted from DES, 1988, Table C16)
Note: 'Biology' here includes passes in botany and zoology

subjects, at two levels: the higher level is GCE A level, and the lower level is a combination of CSE, GCE O level and GCSE. (This is because 1988 was a transitional year from GCE and CSE to GCSE. See Chapter 9.)

By the sixth form, a pattern is well established of arts subjects (especially languages) being 'girls' subjects', and maths and sciences (other than

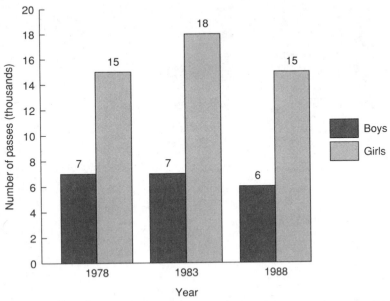

Figure 11.7   A level passes in French and other modern languages held by school leavers, England 1978–88
(Adapted from DES, 1980, Table 13; 1983, Table C13; 1988, Table C16)

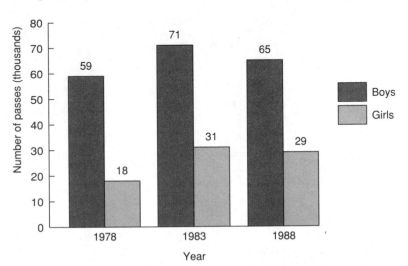

Figure 11.8   A level passes in maths, physics and chemistry held by school leavers, England 1978–88
(Adapted from DES, 1980, Table 13; 1983, Table C13; 1988, Table C16)

biology) being 'boys' subjects'. Figures 11.7 and 11.8 show how these patterns have been reflected during the past decade, in England, in A level passes held by school leavers.

These differences remain, despite a swing by girls towards maths and science in the 1970s and 1980s. In 1970, the three most common A levels awarded to girls were English, history and French; by 1985, they were English, biology and maths. For boys, the three most common remained maths, physics and chemistry throughout this period (DES, 1972, Table 32; 1988, Table C16).

Participation in higher education also shows overall differences between the sexes, though here it is men who predominate. In 1987–8, there were 570,000 men and 423,000 women in higher education in the United Kingdom (full- and part-time, universities, polytechnics and colleges). However, the gap between the sexes is narrowing: men now make up 57% of students in higher education, compared with 63% in 1980–1 and 67% in 1970–1 (Government Statistical Service, 1989, Table 27).

The discrepancy between men and women is greater at higher degree level than at first degree level. This is illustrated by Figure 11.9, which shows the numbers of degrees of various types obtained by full-time university students in 1987.

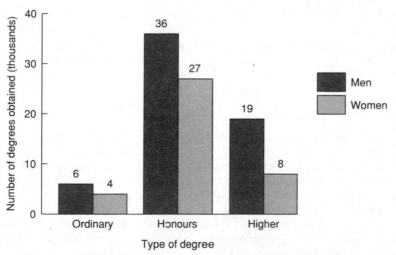

Figure 11.9 Numbers of men and women obtaining different types of degree, full-time university students, United Kingdom 1987 (Adapted from CSO, 1990, Table 5.17)

As with schools, though, these global figures conceal great variation from subject to subject. Figure 11.10 shows the numbers of university courses, in different subject areas, taken by men and by women in the United Kingdom in the academic year 1987–8. (These figures do not include Open University courses.)

Differences between the sexes in education patterns are also discussed

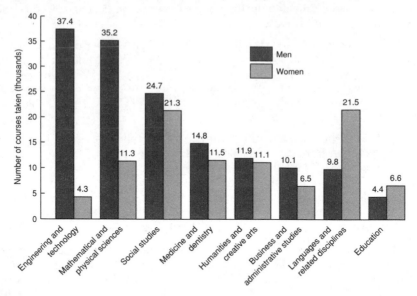

Figure 11.10   Numbers of men and women taking selected university courses (other than Open University), United Kingdom 1984–5 (Adapted from CSO, 1990, Table 5.16)

below in the sections on independent and special schools. For differences in pattern of employment in educational institutions, see Chapter 7.

Ethnic groups

Information about educational differences and similarities between ethnic groups is more scarce, less recent and less reliable than that available for the sexes. Ethnic divisions are not categories used in the national collection and publication of official statistics on education (though this is to change from 1990–1); data have to be taken from sample surveys. Most of the information below is taken from surveys conducted for the Rampton/ Swann Committee (see Chapter 3: 1981 Rampton; 1985 Swann), in 1979 and 1982, in five LEAs with high proportions of ethnic minority pupils. All five LEAs were inner city areas, where the average educational attainment for *every* ethnic group is lower than the national average.

Children and young people from different ethnic groups show differences in educational attainment: white and Asian children and young people achieve higher results, on average, than Afro-Caribbean, as Figure 11.11 illustrates.

However, this picture needs to be qualified in a number of ways.

First, different ethnic groups are often of very different social class composition (see Chapter 2, Figure 2.14). Since educational attainment is strongly linked to social class (see below), some of the ostensible differ-

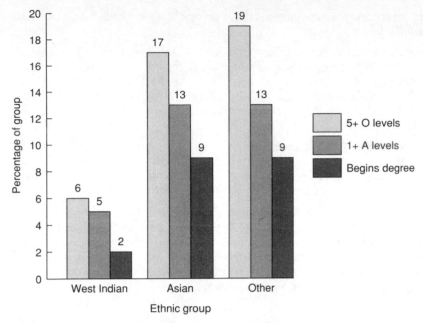

*Figure 11.11   Educational attainment of different ethnic groups, 1981–2
(Adapted from DES, 1985, Chapter 3)*

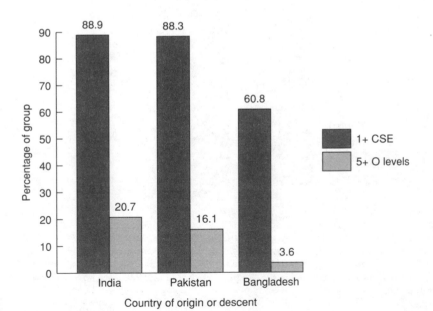

*Figure 11.12   Examination results of fifth-year Asian pupils in the ILEA, by
country of origin or descent, 1986
(Adapted from ILEA Research and Statistics, 1987, Table 6)
Note: '1+CSE' means at least one CSE grade 5 or higher; '5+O levels' means at least
five O levels grade C or higher*

ences in achievement between ethnic groups may be reflections of these class differences.

Secondly, none of these ethnic categories are monolithic. The 'Asian' group, for example, is itself made up of groups of different levels of achievement. This is illustrated by data from the ILEA in Figure 11.12, which compares the examination results of fifth-year pupils of Indian, Pakistani and Bangladeshi origin or descent.

Thirdly, data collected by the Inner London Education Authority (which published more detailed statistics than central government or other LEAs on differences between ethnic groups) have shown Asian pupils as having distinctly higher average educational attainment than white or Afro-Caribbean pupils (see, e.g., ILEA Research and Statistics, 1987).

Finally, the Rampton/Swann statistics themselves provide evidence that the educational achievements of Afro-Caribbean children and young people are increasing from year to year at a higher rate than those of other groups. Figure 11.13 compares A level results in 1979 (when data were gathered for the Rampton Report) with those in 1982 (when comparable data were collected for the Swann Report).

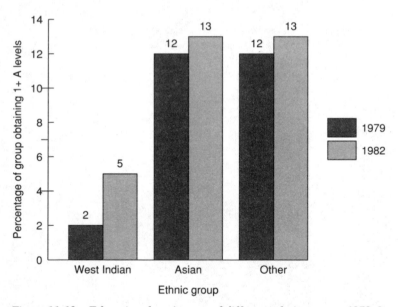

Figure 11.13   Educational attainment of different ethnic groups, 1978–9 and 1981–2 (Adapted from DES, 1981, Chapter 1, Table D; DES, 1985a, Chapter 3, Annex B) Note: There is a minor discrepancy between the 1978–9 figures for Asians as given in the Rampton Report (13%) and in the Swann Report (12%). Here we have followed Swann

Differences between ethnic groups in education patterns are also discussed in the section on special needs. For differences in patterns of employment in educational institutions, see Chapter 7.

Social class

Although social class is one of the census categories (see Chapter 2), it is not widely used in the publication of official statistics on education. Nor have there been many recent sample-survey investigations of the relationship between social class and educational attainment. One reason for this relative neglect may be that so many earlier surveys gave such clear and unequivocal results: at virtually every stage of education, by virtually every criterion of achievement, middle-class children had higher levels of achievement than working-class children. This was documented particularly thoroughly in surveys conducted for a succession of official reports in the 1950s and 1960s (see Chapter 3, especially 1954 Gurney-Dixon, 1959 Crowther, 1963 Newsom, 1963–4 Robbins and 1967 Plowden), whose criteria of educational achievement ranged from 11 plus passes to class of university degree.

In the 1950s and 1960s, most of those surveyed were, or had been, at school under the tripartite system. There has been little research in most of

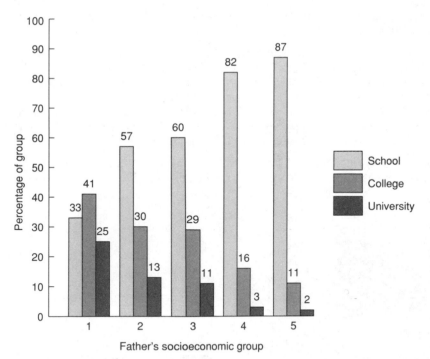

Figure 11.14 Last educational establishment attended full-time, by father's socioeconomic group, Great Britain 1986–7
(Adapted from OPCS, 1989, Table 10.6a)
Key to socioeconomic groups: 1 Professional; 2 Employers and managers; 3 Intermediate and junior non-manual; 4 Skilled manual and self-employed non-professional; 5 Semi-skilled and unskilled manual
Note: Categories 3 and 5 each combine two OPCS categories; 'college' includes polytechnics and colleges of further education

the United Kingdom into the relative effects of social class on achievement under the tripartite and comprehensive systems. In Scotland, however, while differences between the social classes in educational attainment remain, they are smaller in the comprehensive system than they were in the tripartite. The trend towards equality of attainment is especially marked in schools that have been comprehensive for a long time. It has been a result of the raising of working-class attainment, not the lowering of middle-class attainment (McPherson and Willms, 1987).

Such recent survey evidence as exists for Great Britain as a whole shows that, whatever the effects of comprehensivisation, the link between social class and educational achievement remains strong. For example, Figure 11.14 shows, for adults in Great Britain aged 25–49 in 1986–7, the relationship between their fathers' socioeconomic groups (as defined by the OPCS) and the last educational establishment they attended full-time. Roughly speaking, the lower the socioeconomic group of someone's father, the more likely it is that his or her full-time education ended in school, rather than college or university.

However, the number of people with fathers in the professional group is relatively small, so that they are still a minority of those who have been in higher education. Figure 11.15 illustrates this (from the same sample) for universities.

The likelihood that a person enters higher education continues to be strongly related to his or her family's social class. In Great Britain in 1987, 62% of students in universities and polytechnics had fathers in non-manual occupations, and 38% had fathers in manual occupations. By comparison, 36% of men in the population as a whole were in non-manual occupations and 64% in manual occupations (OPCS, 1989, Tables 9.29 and 10.1. The figure for universities includes Open University students).

People's own occupational level is also strongly related to their level of educational attainment. This is illustrated in Figure 11.16, which shows the

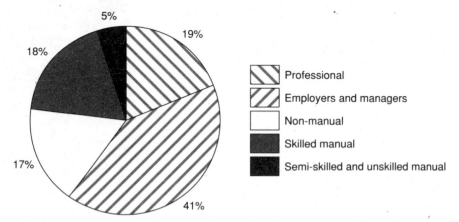

Figure 11.15   Socioeconomic groups of fathers of people whose last full-time education was at university
(Adapted from OPCS, 1989, Table 10.6b)

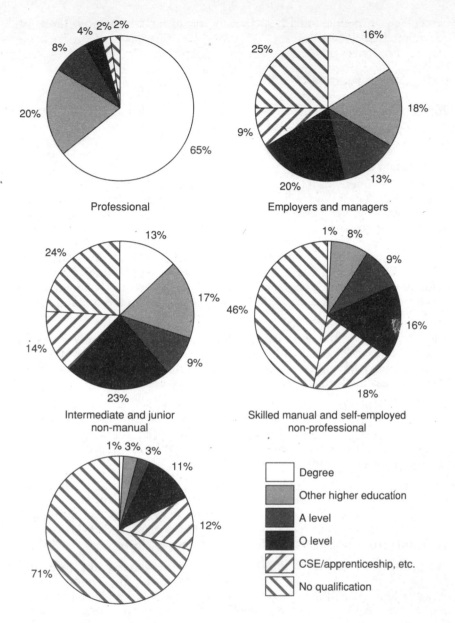

Figure 11.16   Highest qualification shown as percentage of each socioeconomic group, Great Britain 1986–7
(Adapted from OPCS, 1989, Table 10.11a)
Note: CSE grade 1 is counted under 'O level', not under 'CSE'; the figures for 'intermediate and junior non-manual' and for 'semi-skilled and unskilled manual' each combine two OPCS categories; people with qualifications other than those above (e.g. from abroad) are omitted

percentages of people in each socioeconomic group with various levels of educational qualification.

Independent schools

Pupils in independent schools (see Chapter 5) form a small percentage of all school pupils — about 7% of boys, 6% of girls in England and Wales in 1988, which represents a decline from the percentage not long after the war (1951) of 8% of boys (9% if direct grant schools are included). However, independent schools retain a much higher proportion of their pupils after the legal minimum school-leaving age than do maintained schools, so that in 1988, 19% of all boys and 15% of all girls over 16 were in independent schools. This shows a percentage decline since 1951 (when the corresponding figure for boys was 29%, or 38% including direct grant schools); during this period, there was a substantial increase in *absolute* numbers over the minimum leaving age in independent schools, but this was overshadowed by a much larger increase, proportionately as well as absolutely, in maintained schools. (Figures for 1951 have been taken, and rounded, from Halsey, Heath and Ridge, 1984, Table 1; 1988 figures from CSO, 1990, Table 3.12.)

The percentage of pupils in independent schools is significantly lower in Scotland than in England and Wales: under 4% overall and about 9% of pupils over 16 (though there is considerable variation from region to region (1984 figures: Walford, 1987, Table 2).

Fees for independent schools are high. For example, the average annual fees in Headmasters' Conference Schools in 1990 were £6900 for boarders, and £4000 for day pupils. In schools belonging to the Girls' Schools Association, the average annual fees were £6300 for boarders, and £3300 for day pupils (ISIS, 1990).

Approximately 30,000 pupils, 6% of pupils in independent schools in England, hold places under the Assisted Places Scheme, which provides assistance with tuition fees and certain other expenses. A further 67,000 (14%) receive help with fees from the schools themselves, 8000 (2%) from local authorities and 4000 (1%) from other sources (ISIS, 1990, Table 7).

Independent schools have drawn their pupils very unequally from the different social classes, as Figure 11.17 illustrates for the Oxford Social Mobility Study's sample of men in England and Wales who had completed their education by 1972 (women were not included in the study). It shows the percentages of men with fathers in each of the three main social classes identified in the study (see Chapter 2 for explanation of these) who had attended private schools (including direct grant schools).

Pupils in independent schools achieve higher levels of success in public examinations than those at maintained schools. Figure 11.18 shows the percentages of pupils (boys and girls taken together) in each sector gaining three or more A levels (important for university entry), in England and Wales in 1951 and 1981.

Of both boys and girls who gain A level passes, a higher percentage of

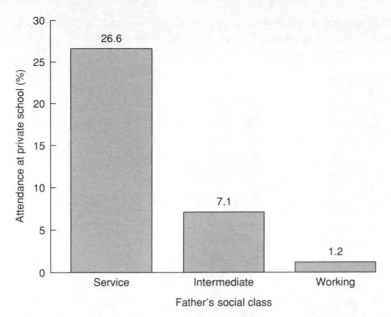

Figure 11.17   Percentages of men of each social class (defined by father's social class) who had attended private school, England and Wales 1972 (Adapted from Halsey, Heath and Ridge, 1980, Table 4.8)

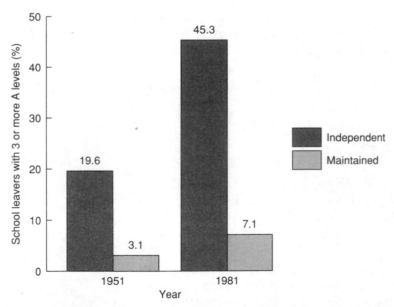

Figure 11.18   Percentage of school leavers from independent and maintained schools with three or more A levels, England and Wales 1951 and 1981 (Adapted from Halsey, Heath and Ridge, 1984, Table 3) Note: The 1951 'independent' figure includes direct grant schools

those in independent schools gain three or more passes than do those in maintained schools, as is shown in Figure 11.19.

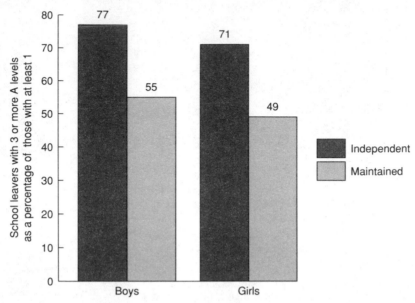

Figure 11.19   Boys and girls in each type of school who have passed three or more A levels as a percentage of those who have passed at least one, England and Wales 1985 (Adapted from OPCS, 1987b, Table 10.1)

At the other extreme, the percentage of pupils leaving school with no qualifications in the same year was lower for independent schools (2%) than for maintained schools (10%) (England, 1985 figures; DES, 1986, Table C3).

Attitudes to private schools are summarised in Figure 11.20, which shows

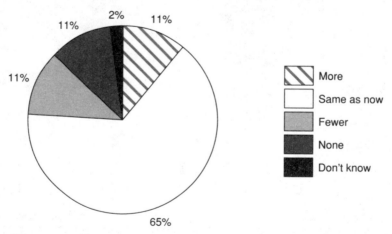

Figure 11.20   Attitudes to private schools (Adapted from Flather, 1988, p. 22)

the percentages of people in Great Britain (in 1987) who thought there should be more, fewer, none, or about the same number as then.

There is little variation with age or sex in these attitudes, but some variation between social classes. Respondents in non-manual occupations are more likely to think that there should be more private schools, or the same number as now, than respondents in manual occupations (77% compared with 62%).

Special needs

Educational provision for children with statements of special educational needs (see Chapter 3, 1978 Warnock; Chapter 4, 1981 Education Act) is varied, and changing over time (see Chapter 5, Figures 5.14–5.16).

Different types of special school frequently cater for all levels of special curriculum need — 'developmental', 'modified' and 'mainstream plus support' (see Chapter 13) — but in different proportions. This is illustrated in Figure 11.21. In addition, some 40,931 pupils with statements are taught

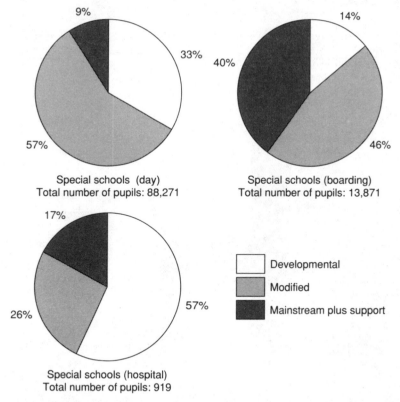

Figure 11.21   Composition of special schools by curriculum need, England January 1988
(Adapted from DES, 1989, Table A23)

in mainstream schools, but no data are published about their specific curriculum needs (DES, 1989, Table A26).

Boys are over-represented and girls under-represented in special schools, as compared with their numbers in the population as a whole; this is illustrated in Figure 11.22 using the data for England.

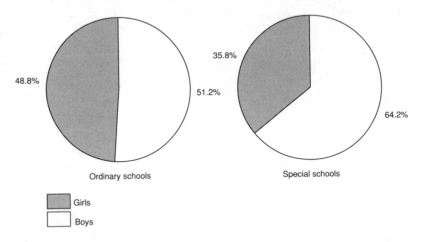

Figure 11.22   Percentages of boys and girls in ordinary and in special schools, England 1988
(Adapted from DES, 1989, Tables A1 and A10)

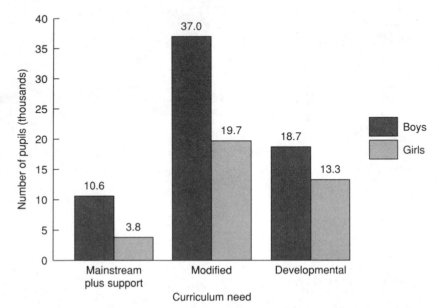

Figure 11.23   Numbers of boys and girls in special schools with different curriculum needs, England 1985
(Adapted from DES, 1989, Table A23)

Differences between boys and girls among special school pupils with particular curriculum needs are shown in Figure 11.23.

In the ILEA (which published much more detailed statistics on special education than central government or other LEAs), boys were in the majority in schools and units catering for every type of special need. They were particularly over-represented in schools catering for children with emotional and behavioural difficulties (87%) and in units for the language impaired (79%) (ILEA Research and Statistics, 1984, Table 2).

The ethnic compositions of ordinary and special schools are compared, again for the ILEA, in Figures 11.24 (primary) and 11.25 (secondary). At both primary and secondary levels, Afro-Caribbean and English/Scottish/Welsh/Irish groups were over-represented in special schools as compared with their numbers in ordinary schools; Asian and 'other' groups were under-represented.

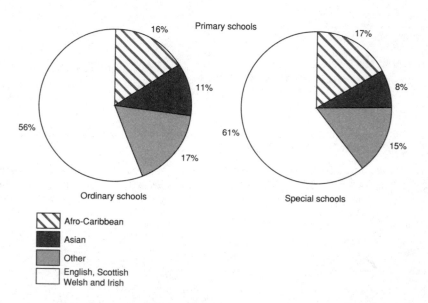

Figure 11.24 Ethnic groups as percentages of the population of ordinary and special primary schools, the ILEA 1984
(Adapted from ILEA Research and Statistics, 1984)

There were a number of differences between ethnic groups in the types of special school or unit that children were likely to attend, but there is no obvious pattern to this variation. The largest single difference is that, of the Asian children in special schools or units, only 1% were in schools catering for children with emotional and behavioural difficulties, compared with 22% of the Afro-Caribbean children and 16% of the English, Scottish, Welsh and Irish children in special schools or units (ILEA Research and Statistics, 1984, Table 2).

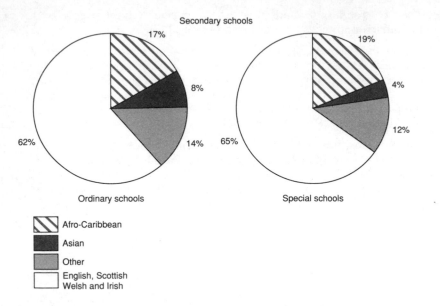

Figure 11.25   Ethnic groups as percentages of the population of ordinary and special secondary schools, the ILEA 1984
(Adapted from ILEA Research and Statistics, 1984)

The first destinations after school of special school pupils are shown, once again for the ILEA, in Figure 11.26.

Further education provision for students with special needs is also varied. In England in 1985, according to a survey conducted for the DES, there were approximately 43,500 students in further education with special

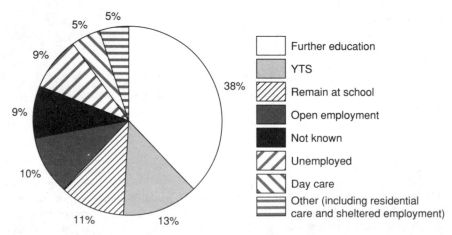

Figure 11.26   First destinations after school of special school pupils, the ILEA day schools 1984)
(Adapted from a survey by Mr Matthew Griffiths of MENCAP)

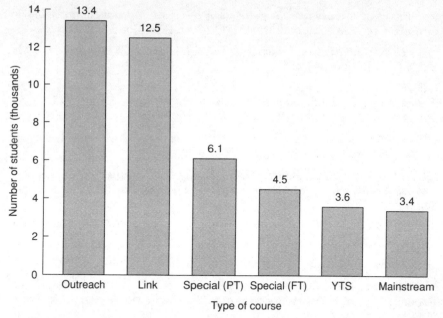

Figure 11.27   Numbers of students with special educational needs on FE courses, England 1985
(Adapted from DES, 1987b)
Note on the type of courses: outreach — course conducted outside an FE college by members of its staff for students not enrolled with the college; link — course conducted by, and at, an FE college for half a day or one day (occasionally two days) per week for students enrolled at another institution (e.g. a hospital or residential centre); special — course, within an FE college, designed for students with special educational needs: may be part-time (PT) or full-time (FT); mainstream — ordinary course in an FE college, not specifically designed for students with special educational needs

educational needs, as defined in the Warnock Report. Of these, just under 8% were on mainstream courses. The distribution of students with special needs among different types of courses is shown in Figure 11.27.

Sources and further reading

CSO (1988) *Social Trends*, No. 18, 1988 edn, London, HMSO.

CSO (1990) *Annual Abstract of Statistics*, No. 126, 1987 edn, London, HMSO.

DES (1972) *Statistics of Education 1970 Vol. 2: School Leavers CSE and GCE*, London, HMSO.

DES (1980) *Statistics of Education 1978 Vol. 2: School Leavers CSE and GCE*, Table 13, London, HMSO.

DES (1981) *West Indian Children in our Schools: Interim Report of the*

Committee of Inquiry into the Education of Children from Ethnic Minority Groups, Cmnd. 8273, London, HMSO ('The Rampton Report').

DES (1983) *Statistics of Education: School Leavers CSE and GCE 1983*, Table C13, London, HMSO.

DES (1985) *Education for All: Report of the Committee of Inquiry into the Education of Children from Ethnic Minority Groups*, Cmnd. 9453, London, HMSO ('The Swann Report').

DES (1986) *Statistics of Education: School Leavers 1986*. London, Department of Education and Science.

DES (1987b) *Statistics Bulletin 7/87: Students in Further Education with Special Needs, November 1985*, London, Department of Education and Science.

DES (1988) *Statistics of Education: School Leavers CSE and GCE 1988*, London, HMSO.

DES (1989) *Statistics of Education: Schools 1988*, London, HMSO.

Flather, P. (1988) Education matters, in Jowell, R., Witherspoon, S. and Brooks, L. (eds) *British Social Attitudes: The 1986 Report*, Aldershot, Gower.

Government Statistical Service (1986) *Educational Statistics for the United Kingdom 1986*, London, HMSO.

Government Statistical Service (1989) *Educational Statistics for the United Kingdom 1989*, London, HMSO.

Halsey, A. H., Heath, A. F. and Ridge, J. M. (1980) *Origins and Destinations: Family, Class and Education in Modern Britain*, Oxford, Clarendon Press.

Halsey, A. H., Heath, A. F. and Ridge, J. M. (1984) The political arithmetic of public schools, in Walford, G. (ed.) *British Public Schools: Policy and Practice*, pp. 9–44, London, Falmer Press.

ILEA Research and Statistics (1984) *Characteristics of Pupils in Special Schools*, RS 962/84, London, Inner London Education Authority.

ILEA Research and Statistics (1987) *Ethnic Background and Examination Results*, RS 1120/87, London, Inner London Education Authority.

ISIS (1990) *Annual Census 1990*, London, Independent Schools Information Service.

McPherson, A. F. and Willms, J. D. (1987) Equalisation and improvement: some effects of comprehensive reorganisation in Scotland, *Sociology*, Vol. 21, No. 4.

OPCS (1987b) *Young People's Intentions to Enter Higher Education: The Report of a Survey Carried Out by the Social Survey Division of OPCS on Behalf of the DES*, London, HMSO.

OPCS (1989) *General Household Survey 1987*, No. 17, London, HMSO.

CHAPTER 12 SCHOOL LEAVERS AND PREPARATION FOR EMPLOYMENT

The percentage of young people staying on in full-time education after the legal minimum leaving age has increased during the last decade, as Figure 12.1 shows. At 16 they are more likely to be studying at school; by 18 they are much more likely to be studying at an establishment of further or higher education.

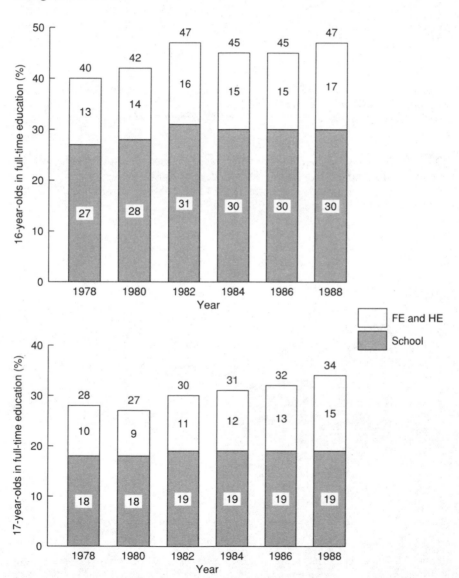

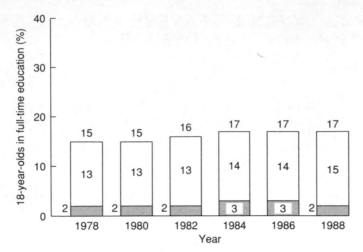

*Figure 12.1   Percentage of 16–18-year-olds in full-time education, England 1978–88
(Adapted from DES, 1988, Tables 2–4)
Note: The category FE and HE excludes YTS (see below) within colleges*

During the same period there has been a significant overall fall in
employment and rise in unemployment, among 16–18-year-olds. This is
illustrated, for England, in Figure 12.2. (The 1988 unemployment figures
show a drop from the peak of 16% in 1983–4.)

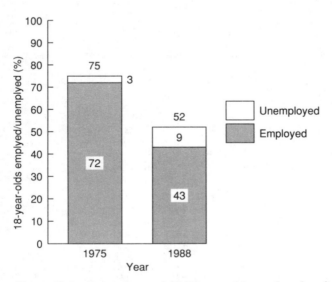

*Figure 12.2   Percentages of 16–18-year-olds employed and unemployed, England
1975 and 1988
(Adapted from DES, 1988, Table 1)
Note: The category 'Unemployed' refers to claimants only. Those not employed but
not seeking work, or seeking work but not claiming benefit, are officially classified as
'In employment'*

Young people, especially school leavers aged 16 and 17, also have a number of training schemes available to them under the auspices of the Department of Employment (formerly the Manpower Services Commission) — some of these operate within the schools and FE colleges described in Chapter 5, others outside. (The Department also runs a number of training schemes for older people.)

Department of Employment Training Schemes

The *Manpower Services Commission* (MSC) was set up in 1973, as a partly autonomous body attached to the Department of Employment, and responsible in England to the Secretary of State for Employment. (Formal resonsibility for the MSC's activities in Scotland and Wales rested after 1978 with the Scottish and Welsh Secretaries of State. The MSC did not operate in Northern Ireland, which has its own training schemes.)

During its existence, the structure and functions of the MSC were subject to virtually continuous review and reorganisation. (For details see CIPFA, no single date, Chapter 12.) Throughout the changes, however, the MSC retained as its main responsibility the provision of vocational education and training, especially for young people and the unemployed; and as its basic structure a central Commission with representatives of employers, trade unions and government, together with networks of local committees which advised on educational and training needs, and of local 'managing agents' (such as employers, FE colleges and LEAs) which ran training programmes under the supervision of the Commission.

In 1988, however, the MSC was disbanded as a separate, semi-autonomous organisation, and its functions were taken over by a new section set up within the Department of Employment, originally called the Training Agency but later renamed the Training, Enterprise and Education Division. Many of its responsibilities are currently being handed over to Training and Enterprise Councils (TECs) — independent companies, consisting mainly of local groups of employers, who will contract with the government to plan and provide training, and promote small businesses and self-employment, in their area. The Training Agency's estimated total expenditure for 1989–90 was £2.5 billion, equivalent to about 10% of the total expenditure of the DES (HM Treasury, 1990, Table 6.3).

The main educational and training schemes of the MSC and its successors include those listed below. (There have also been many smaller schemes: see CIPFA, no single date, Chapter 12; Thomson and Rosenberg, 1986.)

Training Opportunities Scheme (TOPS)
TOPS aimed to meet local skill shortages by training adults as well as young people to meet them. (It ceased operating in 1985.)

Youth Opportunities Programme (YOPS)
YOPS aimed to make young people more employable; some of their training was carried out in colleges, but most at workplaces. (It was replaced in 1983 by the Youth Training Scheme.)

Youth Training Scheme (YTS)/Youth Training (YT)

YTS was introduced in 1983 to replace YOPS, and it is still in operation, although in a revised form. It will itself be replaced in 1990–1 by Youth Training. As currently organised, it combines work experience with 'on-the-job' and 'off-the-job' training for young people leaving school or college, in periods of two years for 16-year-olds, and one year for 17-year-olds. It guarantees a training place to all 16- and 17-year-olds who leave full-time education and cannot find a job. YTS programmes are run by local managing agents — employers, FE colleges or voluntary organisations set up by LEAs — and have been monitored and partly financed by the Training Agency; the rest of the costs of the training programmes are to be met by contributions from local employers. There are no nationally fixed levels for training fees or charges to employers. As TECs develop, they will take over the provision of Youth Training.

FACT

In 1989–90, 281,000 young people, 57% of all 16- and 17-year-old school leavers, joined a YTS/YT scheme; an estimated 50% of those leaving YTS/YT gained a qualification; and 83% of those leaving YTS/YT went into jobs or further education or training. YTS/YT incurred £1 billion expenditure in 1989–90, 40% of the total annual expenditure of the Training Agency (HM Treasury, 1990, Tables 6.3 and 6.5).

Similar numbers of people are expected to join YT schemes each year until 1992–3, but as employers progressively take over from the government, its

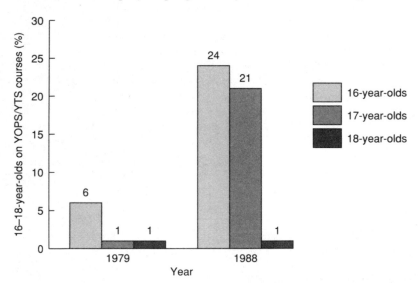

Figure 12.3   Percentages of 16–18-year-olds on YOPS/YTS courses, England 1979 and 1988
(Adapted from DES, 1988, Tables 2–4)

annual expenditure on YT is expected to fall — to some £760 million in 1992–3 (HM Treasury, 1990, Table 6.5). Figure 12.3 shows the growth in numbers of young people taking vocational training between 1979 (on YOPS) and 1988 (on YTS) as percentages of the population of different ages. As a result of recent reorganisation of the YTS scheme, there was a large increase among 16- and 17-year-olds, and the very small percentage of 18-year-olds on YOPS courses continued on YTS courses.

Youth Training Programme (YTP)
YTP is the Northern Ireland equivalent of the YTS, but has been the joint responsibility of the Northern Ireland Departments of Economic Development and of Education, not the MSC or the Training Agency. From April 1990, it is the responsibility of the new Training and Employment Agency – a Northern Ireland equivalent of the Training Agency. YTP offers full-time training places on a two-year programme to all 16- and 17-year-old school leavers, combining work experience, vocational training and further education. In 1989–90, 16,000 people entered the Programme, and 10,700 gained a qualification. For 1990–1, £33 million have been allocated to YTP (HM Treasury, 1990, Table 17.9).

Employment Training (ET)
ET was introduced in September 1988, and replaces the Job Training Scheme. It is intended for long-term unemployed adults (and other adults with particular difficulties in finding work, such as disabilities) and aims to help them acquire skills and return to employment. It guarantees a place to anyone aged 18 to 25 who has been unemployed for over six months, and attempts to offer a place to anyone up to 50 who has been unemployed for over two years. (In the event, 15% of ET trainees in its first year of operation were from the former group, and 33% from the latter.)

Expenditure on ET in 1989–90 is an estimated £1.1 billion, slightly more than on YTS/YT. At any one time, some 200,000 people were in the ET programme. Trainees are given the opportunity to work towards a recognised vocational qualification (15% of those leaving ET in 1989–90 had acquired one), and are paid an allowance of £10 a week more than their benefit entitlement (HM Treasury, 1990, Table 6.6).

Job Training Programme (JTP)
JTP is the Northern Ireland equivalent of ET, and is under the auspices of the Training and Employment Agency. In 1989, there were over 1000 long-term unemployed people on the Programme: this figure was planned to rise to 2000 in 1990 and over 3000 in 1991. £10 million have been allocated to JTP for 1990–1 (HM Treasury, 1990, Chapter 17, Paras 44–5).

Technical and Vocational Education Initiative (TVEI)
TVEI is a scheme whereby LEAs receive grants for approved programmes of technical and vocational education for 14–18-year-olds in schools and colleges. The TVEI was set up in 1983 as a series of pilot projects designed to test a variety of different methods and approaches, and was extended in 1987, becoming a national scheme intended, eventually, to be available to all 14–18-year-olds, irrespective of ability.

FACT

By 1989–90, all LEAs had taken part in TVEI programmes as part of the pilot scheme, and the national scheme had extended to 67% of LEAs and 55% of schools and colleges, with 30% of the age group taking part (HM Treasury, 1990, Table 6.8).

Spending on TVEI in 1989–90 was estimated at £117 million, approximately 4.7% of the Training Agency's budget.

Work-related further education (WRFE)

In 1985–6, the government transferred a quarter of the overall funding for work-related FE courses in further education colleges from local authorities' budgets (by deducting it from the rate support grant, the predecessor of the revenue support grant; see Chapter 8) to the MSC. Initially, each authority received back from the MSC, for WRFE, a sum roughly equal to the amount deducted from its grant. But to obtain these funds now, all local authorities have to submit three-year plans for their provision of WRFE, for approval by the Department of Employment in the light of its judgement about training needs and appropriate methods of meeting them. The Department's share of the costs of approved courses was intended to average out at 25%. In 1989–90, the Training Agency's share of expenditure on WRFE was an estimated £112 million.

The division of the Training Agency's expenditure among its major schemes in 1989–90 is shown in Figure 12.4.

Figure 5.19 in Chapter 5 summarises the main institutions offering further and higher education, and illustrates some of the available routes that schools leavers might follow. Figure 12.5 shows the actual educational and economic activity of 16-, 17- and 18-year-olds, male and female, in England today.

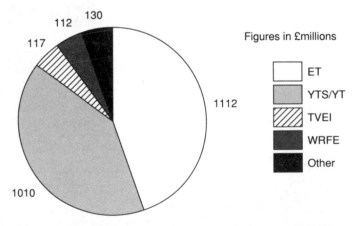

Figure 12.4   Estimated expenditure of the Training Agency, 1989–90 (Adapted from HM Treasury, 1990, Tables 6.3–6.11)

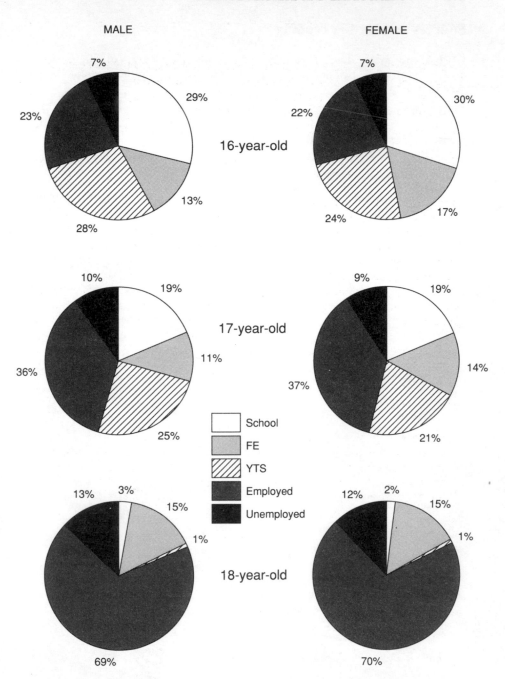

Figure 12.5   Educational and economic activity of 16–18-year-old men and women,
England 1988
(Adapted from DES, 1988, Tables 2–4)
Note: The category 'Unemployed' refers to claimants only. Those not employed but
not seeking work, or seeking work but not claiming benefit, are classified as
'Employed'; the category 'FE' refers to those in full-time further education, including
higher education

Sources and further reading

CIPFA (no single date) *Financial Information Services*, Vol. 20, *Education*, Chapter 12, London, Chartered Institute of Public Finance and Accountancy.

DES (1988) *Statistical Bulletin 14/88: Educational and Economic Activity of Young People aged 16 to 18 years in England from 1975 to 1986*, London, Department of Education and Science.

HM Treasury (1990) *The Government's Expenditure Plans 1990–91 to 1992–93*, London, HMSO.

Thomson, A. and Rosenberg, H. (1986) *A User's Guide to the Manpower Services Commission*, London, Kogan Page.

CHAPTER 13 GLOSSARY OF EDUCATIONAL TERMS

Aided School

type of voluntary school where the voluntary body retains control over the employment of teachers, religious instruction and admissions policy, in exchange for meeting part of the external maintenance costs

Ancillary Staff

non-teaching staff in schools (e.g. laboratory assistants, caretakers, secretaries) and unqualified classroom assistants

Assessment of Performance Unit

section of the DES which monitors the performance of children at different stages of their education

Assisted Places Scheme

a scheme introduced in the 1980 Education Act whereby central government pays part of the tuition costs (on a means-tested basis) for children who have been in state schools to attend selected independent day schools

Banding

modified form of streaming, where pupils are divided into broad bands of ability (e.g. average, below average, above average) and each band follows a similar curriculum

Burnham Committee/ Burnham Scale

until its abolition in 1987, a national committee composed of teachers' unions and local authority employers, which negotiated teachers' salaries on the basis of the 'Burnham Scale' (also abolished), in which teaching jobs were graded from scale 1 (the lowest) to scale 4

Capping

mechanism by which central government sets limits to the amount of money a local authority is allowed to raise through the Community Charge

Catchment Area

geographical area around a school, defined by the LEA, which gives pupils living there the right to attend that school

Central Institution

Scottish institution for higher education, similar to the English polytechnic

City Technology College

school with a technological bias, set up by private sponsors with government grants

Community Home	replaced approved schools under the 1969 Children and Young Persons Act. Administered by Social Services Departments
Comprehensive School	secondary school which does not select children for admission on the grounds of ability
Consortium	group of schools which join together for a particular purpose, for example to purchase equipment or to teach certain subjects (especially at fifth- and sixth-form level, where falling rolls would otherwise result in sixth-form groups being too small)
Continuous Assessment	judging students on the basis of work done during a course rather than, or in addition to, a formal examination at the end
Controlled School	in Great Britain, a type of voluntary school where all costs are met by the LEA but the voluntary body retains some rights over religious instruction. In Northern Ireland, a school financed and managed by an Education and Library Board
'Crammer'	private institution providing intensive coaching for examinations
Curriculum	course of study followed by a pupil or student
Developmental Curriculum	a type of curriculum deemed suitable for children with severe learning difficulties. It has closely defined educational and social objectives, and aims to encourage a degree of personal autonomy (see also Mainstream plus Support Curriculum; Modified Curriculum)
Dyslexia	disability in using and interpreting written language and symbols, irrespective of general intelligence and spoken language skills. (Its existence is widely, but not universally, accepted by educational psychologists and LEAs.)
Education Authority	the Scottish term for a local educational authority. As in England and Wales, EAs form part of the local government structure
Education and Library Board	in Northern Ireland, one of the five regional educational authorities, centrally appointed by the Department of Education for Northern Ireland, though partly consisting of local council

representatives. It is funded by the DENI. It has complete responsibility for controlled schools and is responsible for some services to all schools in its geographical area

Education Otherwise an organisation offering support and help to parents wishing to educate their children out of school (the name is based on a phrase in the 1944 Education Act)

Education Support Grant sum of money earmarked in the Government's Revenue Support Grant for specific projects which the Secretary of State has decided are important, e.g. science teaching in primary schools. LEAs then bid for this money

Educational Priority Area term suggested in the Plowden Report to describe areas of particular social deprivation that should receive extra educational funding

First School primary school taking children from age 5 up to the age of transfer to middle school at 8 or 9

Governor elected or co-opted member of the governing body which every school is now required to have (primary school governors used to be called managers)

Grammar School in the tripartite system in England and Wales, a secondary school taking only children of high academic ability, usually measured by a test taken at age 11 (the tripartite system is now largely replaced, in Great Britain, by comprehensive schools)

Initial Teaching Alphabet a 44-letter phonetic alphabet with only one sound per letter, developed to help children learn to read. Popular in the 1960s but now little used

Inner London Education Authority until April 1990, the largest LEA in the UK, responsible for schools and colleges in the inner London boroughs. With the abolition of the Greater London Council, the ILEA became the only LEA whose members were directly elected, rather than being part of the local government system. It was itself abolished by the 1988 Education Reform Act

Integration the education of children with special educational needs alongside their peers in ordinary, rather than special, schools. The

	term is also used in Northern Ireland to refer to education without denominational segregation
Intermediate Treatment	a form of provision dating from the Children and Young Persons Act (1969) for children deemed to be at risk and in trouble, which often includes persistent truants and pupils whom schools are unable to contain. Run by social services, but LEAs may provide teachers
Junior Secondary School	the Scottish equivalent of the secondary modern school in England and Wales
Local Education Authority	in England and Wales, part of the local government structure, responsible for the day-to-day running of the state education service in a particular geographical area (for Northern Ireland, see Education and Library Board)
Mainstream	an ordinary, rather than a special, school, class, etc. (in America, the term 'mainstreaming' is the equivalent of 'integration')
Mainstream plus Support Curriculum	a type of curriculum deemed suitable for children with particular kinds of special need. As the name suggests, this is comparable to ordinary curricula in aims, content and standards, but with support appropriate for pupils' distinctive needs — whether in organisation, equipment or style of teaching (see also Modified Curriculum; Developmental Curriculum)
Maintained School	in Great Britain, a school maintained by the state (see also Voluntary Schools). In Northern Ireland, a school provided by the Roman Catholic Church, though with a large measure of state support and controlled by the Maintained Schools Commission (similar to an aided school in Great Britain)
Manpower Services Commission	until 1988, attached to the Department of Employment. Involved in vocational education in schools and FE colleges. Responsible for the development of TVEI schemes in schools and the Youth Training Scheme for school leavers. Now replaced by the Training, Employment and Enterprise Division
Middle School	comprehensive school catering for children aged from 8 to 9 to 12 or 13. Legally

	designated as either primary or secondary depending on whether most children are under or over age 11. Confined almost entirely to England
Modified Curriculum	a type of curriculum deemed suitable for children with moderate learning difficulties. Similar to ordinary school curricula, but with objectives suited to the children's special needs (see also Mainstream plus Support Curriculum; Developmental Curriculum)
National Curriculum	a set of 'essential subjects' which the government decides all children must study, with their performance assessed against set criteria at various ages. At present, applies to England and Wales and, with modifications, to Northern Ireland (see Northern Ireland Curriculum)
Northern Ireland Curriculum	the Northern Ireland equivalent of the English and Welsh National Curriculum
Open Tech	not an institution, but a range of distance learning materials on technical and business subjects, being developed by various institutions with funding from the MSC. Ceased operating in 1987
Peripatetic Teacher	visiting teacher, i.e. one who is not attached to any one school but travels to several (e.g. to teach music or to give specialist help for deaf children)
Pooling	mechanism for sharing expenses between LEAs on services which may be used by all authorities but are concentrated in a few, e.g. the advanced further education pool for polytechnics and college of higher education
Portage	scheme first developed in Portage, USA, to help parents teach their handicapped child at home before he or she starts school, by working on an agreed programme with a trained home visitor
Preparatory School	private, fee-charging school for children between the ages of 8 and 11 (girls) or 13 (boys), preparing children for entrance examinations for the independent secondary and public schools
Public School	usually used, especially in England, to refer to one of the prestigious independent schools for boys. In Scotland, however,

'public school' refers to a maintained school

Pupil Profile
form of evaluation designed to give more detailed information about a pupil than an examination result. It may include academic grades, but also such things as internal school assessments, material selected by the pupil and teachers' comments

Reception Class
the first class of an infant or first school, taking children at (or before) the age of five

Revenue Support Grant
money allocated to local authorities by the government to supplement the local Community Charge. Each authority decides what proportion to spend on education

Rising Fives
children who are not yet five years old, admitted to schools in the term before their fifth birthday, or in some areas at the beginning of the school year in which they will become five

Sandwich Course
course with periods of study at a university, polytechnic or college, alternating with periods of training and experience in industry, commerce or the professions

Secondary Intermediate School
the Northern Ireland equivalent of the secondary modern school in England and Wales

Secondary Modern School
in the tripartite system in England and Wales, a secondary school which caters for those children, identified as of average and below average academic ability, who do not go to grammar schools. (The tripartite system is now largely replaced, in Great Britain, by comprehensive schools)

Section 5 Letter
the letter sent by the LEA to parents to inform them that the authority intends to begin the full assessment procedure to determine a child's special educational needs — a procedure begun when it has been decided that the child's needs cannot be met within the ordinary resources of the school. ('Section 5' refers to the relevant part of the 1981 Education Act and means that the procedure was initiated by the LEA; parents themselves can also initiate the procedure, under Section 9 of the Act)

Senior Secondary School	the Scottish equivalent of the grammar school in England and Wales
Setting	grouping pupils according to ability in a particular subject. A student may thus be in one set for English, another for mathematics, etc.
Sixth Form College	separate school for 16–19-year-olds, taking pupils from several schools in an area
Special Agreement School	type of secondary school with similar rights and responsibilities to an aided school. Set up by a special agreement for joint provision made between a voluntary body and an LEA before the 1944 Education Act
Special Educational Needs	term introduced by the Warnock Report to replace the old categories of handicap
Special School	separate school for children with mental, physical or emotional difficulties
Statement	formal document drawn up by an LEA (in consultation with parents) describing the special educational needs of a child who needs more help than can be provided within the ordinary resources of a school. The assessment procedure leading to a statement is laid down in the 1981 Education Act
Streaming	allocating pupils, on the basis of perceived ability, to 'streams', i.e. classes in which pupils stay for all subjects, usually following different curricula
Supply Teacher	teacher appointed by an LEA to fill in for absent school staff, for periods ranging from half a day to several weeks
Teacher Placement Service	government-funded scheme operating in England, Wales and Scotland to support short-term teacher placements in industry, business, and the public sector
Technical and Vocational Education Initiative	scheme funded by the Department of Employment for schools and colleges to develop their own work-related courses for pupils between the ages of 14 and 18. Introduced as an experimental scheme in 1983, extended in 1987 to all English and Welsh LEAs.
Tertiary College	college for young people over the age of 16 that combines the functions of a sixth form and FE colleges by offering a full range of academic and vocational courses

Training, Employment and Enterprise Division (formerly, Training Agency) replacement for the Manpower Services Commission. Now an integral part of the Department of Employment

Training and Employment Agency the Northern Ireland equivalent of the Training Agency in Britain

Twenty-one-hour Rule rule enabling claimants of Unemployment or Supplementary Benefit to take part-time further education courses, provided that these do not exceed 21 hours a week, and that the claimant remains 'available for work'

Upper School comprehensive school taking children after they have left a middle school at 12 or 13. (Some secondary schools also use the term to describe the senior half of the school, as opposed to the 'lower school' comprising the first, second and third years)

Urban Programme administered by the Department of the Environment. Some grants are given for educational purposes, e.g. setting up nurseries in deprived areas

Vocational Education employment-related rather than academic education

Voluntary School school provided by a voluntary body (usually the church) but maintained by the LEA in England and Wales, and partly aided by the DENI in Northern Ireland (see Aided, Controlled and Special Agreement Schools)

Youth Training Programme the Northern Ireland equivalent of the Youth Training Scheme

Youth Training Scheme two-year training programme in Great Britain for school leavers, combining education and work experience. Run by the Department of Employment. Trainees are paid a small allowance. In Northern Ireland, the equivalent scheme is called the Youth Training Programme, and is run jointly by the Departments of Economic Development and Education. From September 1988, 16- and 17-year-olds who choose not to take a YTS/YTP course are not eligible for welfare benefit payments (to be replaced in 1991 by Youth Training)

CHAPTER 14 ACRONYMS AND ABBREVIATIONS

The use of acronyms and abbreviations is extremely widespread in writings about education; this chapter contains only a highly selective list of some of the most common and most important.

ACE	Advisory Centre for Education
AEB	Associated Examining Board
AFE	Advanced Further Education
AMA	Association of Metropolitan Authorities
AMMA	Assistant Masters and Mistresses Association
APS	Assisted Places Scheme
APT	Association of Polytechnic Teachers
APU	Assessment of Performance Unit
AS	Advanced Supplementary (examination)
ATC	Accredited Training Centre (for YTS supervisor training) *or* Adult Training Centre
AUT	Association of University Teachers
BA	Bachelor of Arts
BACIE	British Association for Commercial and Industrial Education
BACIFHE	British Accredition Council for Independent Further and Higher Education
BD	Bachelor of Divinity
BEd	Bachelor of Education
BERA	British Educational Research Association
BLitt	Bachelor of Letters
BPhil	Bachelor of Philosophy
BPS	British Psychological Society
BSc	Bachelor of Science
BSL	British Sign Language
BTEC	Business and Technician Education Council
CACE	Central Advisory Council for Education
CAL	Computer Assisted Learning
CASE	Campaign for the Advancement of State Education
CAT	College of Advanced Technology
CDT	Craft, Design and Technology
CE2L	Centre for Teaching English as a Second Language
CEE	Certificate of Extended Education

CEO	Chief Education Officer
CGLI	City and Guilds of London Institute
CHES	Child Health Education Study
CIPFA	Chartered Institute of Public Finance and Accountancy
CNAA	Council for National Academic Awards
COPE	Committee on Primary Education (Scotland)
COSE	Committee on Secondary Education (Scotland)
CPVE	Certificate of Pre-vocational Education
CQSW	Certificate of Qualification in Social Work
CRAC	Careers Research and Advisory Centre
CRE	Commission for Racial Equality
CSE	Certificate of Secondary Education
CSO	Central Statistical Office
CSYS	Certificate of Sixth Year Studies (Scotland)
CTC	City Technology College
CVCP	Committee of Vice Chancellors and Principals of the Universities of the United Kingdom
DD	Doctor of Divinity
DENI	Department of Education Northern Ireland
DES	Department of Education and Science
DHSS	Department of Health and Social Security
DipHE	Diploma in Higher Education
DLitt	Doctor of Letters
DPhil	Doctor of Philosophy
DSc	Doctor of Science
EATE	Economic Awareness in Teacher Education
EBD	Emotional and Behavioural Difficulties
ECATT	Economic Awareness and the Training of Teachers
EFL	English as a Foreign Language
EIS	Educational Institute of Scotland
EOC	Equal Opportunities Commission
EPA	Educational Priority Area
ERA	Educational Reform Act (of 1988)
ERIC	Educational Resources Information Centre
ESG	Education Support Grant
ESL	English as a Second Language
ESN	Educationally Subnormal. **ESN (M)** = moderate. **ESN (S)** = severe. (No longer used)
ET	Employment Training
EWO	Education Welfare Officer

FE	Further Education
FTE	Full-time Equivalent
GAMMA	Girls and Mathematics Association
GBA	Governing Bodies Association (of boys' public schools)
GBGSA	Governing Bodies of Girls' Schools Association
GCE	General Certificate of Education
GCSE	General Certificate of Secondary Education
GERBIL	'Great Education Reform Bill' (widely used as an unofficial acronym for the 1988 Education Reform Bill)
GIST	Girls into Science and Technology
GPDST	Girls' Public Day School Trust
GRE	Grant-related Entitlement
GRIST	Grant-related In-service Training (widely used as an unofficial acronym for LEATGS)
GSA	Girls' Schools Association
HE	Higher Education
HMC	Headmasters' Conference
HMI	Her Majesty's Inspector (or Inspectorate)
HMSO	Her Majesty's Stationery Office
HNC	Higher National Certificate
HND	Higher National Diploma
IAPS	Incorporated Association of Preparatory Schools
ILEA	Inner London Education Authority
INSET	In-service Education of Teachers
IQ	Intelligence Quotient
ISAI	Independent Schools Association Incorporated
ISIS	Independent Schools Information Service
IT	Information Technology *or* Intermediate Treatment
ITA	Initial Teaching Alphabet
ITB	Industrial Training Board
JBPVE	Joint Board for Pre-vocational Education
JTS	Job Training Scheme
LAPP	Lower Attaining Pupils Programme
LCCI	London Chamber of Commerce and Industry
LEA	Local Education Authority
LEATGS	Local Education Authorities Training Grants Scheme
LFM	Local Financial Management
LIB	Bachelor of Laws
LID	Doctor of Laws

LMS	Local Management of Schools
MA	Master of Arts
MBA	Master of Business Administration
MEd	Master of Education
MESP	Mini Enterprise in Schools Project
MLD	Moderate Learning Difficulties
MLitt	Master of Letters
MPhil	Master of Philosophy
MSc	Master of Science
MSC	Manpower Services Commission
NAB	National Advisory Body for Public Sector Higher Education (England)
NAFE	Non-advanced Further Education
NAGM	National Association of Governors and Managers
NAHT	National Association of Head Teachers
NAME	National Antiracist Movement in Education (formerly National Association for Multiracial Education)
NAS/UWT	National Association of Schoolmasters/Union of Women Teachers
NATE	National Association for the Teaching of English
NATFHE	National Association of Teachers in Further and Higher Education
NCB	National Children's Bureau
NCDS	National Child Development Study
NCDT	National Council for Drama Training
NCES	National Council for Educational Standards
NCVQ	National Council for Vocational Qualifications
NEC	National Extension College
NFER	National Foundation for Educational Research
NICED	Northern Ireland Council for Educational Development
NICER	Northern Ireland Council for Educational Research
NNEB	National Nursery Examination Board
NUS	National Union of Students
NUSS	National Union of School Students
NUT	National Union of Teachers
NVQ	National Vocational Qualification
OECD	Organisation for Economic Co-operation and Development
ONC	Ordinary National Certificate
OND	Ordinary National Diploma
OPCS	Office of Population Censuses and Surveys
OU	Open University

PAT	Professional Association of Teachers
PCFC	Polytechnics and Colleges Funding Council
PGCE	Postgraduate Certificate of Education
PhD	Doctor of Philosophy
PICKUP	Professional Industrial and Commercial Updating
PPA	Preschool Playgroups Association
PTA	Parent–Teacher Association
PTR	Pupil/Teacher Ratio
REB	Regional Examining Body
ROSLA	Raising of the School Leaving Age
RSA	Royal Society of Arts
RSG	Rate Support Grant
SATRO	Science and Technology Regional Organisation
SCDC	Schools Curriculum Development Committee
SCE	Scottish Certificate of Education
SCIP	School Curriculum Industry Project
SCOTVEC	Scottish Vocational Education Council
SEC	Secondary Examinations Council
SED	Scottish Education Department
SEN	Special Educational Needs
SEO	Society of Education Officers
SHA	Secondary Heads Association
SHMIS	Society of Headmasters of Independent Schools
SILO	Schools Industry Liaison Officer
SLD	Severe Learning Difficulties
SMP	School Mathematics Project
SSTA	Scottish Secondary Teachers Association
STOPP	Society of Teachers Opposed to Physical Punishment
TEC	Training and Enterprise Council
TEFL	Teaching English as a Foreign Language
TES	*Times Education Supplement*
TESL	Teaching English as a Second Language
TESOL	Teaching of English to Speakers of Other Languages
THES	*Times Higher Education Supplement*
TOPS	Training Opportunities Programme
TPO	Teacher Placement Organiser
TPS	Teacher Placement Service
TVEI	Technical and Vocational Education Initiative
UBI	Understanding British Industry
UCCA	Universities Central Council on Admissions

UFC	Universities Funding Council (to replace **UGC** — University Grants Committee)
UGC	University Grants Committee (to be replaced by **UFC** — Universities Funding Council)
UNESCO	United Nations Educational, Scientific and Cultural Organisation
VC	Vice Chancellor
WAB	Welsh Advisory Board for Public Sector Higher Education
WEA	Workers' Educational Association
WISE	Women into Science and Engineering
WOW	Wider Opportunities for Women
WRFE	Work Related Further Education
YOP	Youth Opportunities Programme
YT	Youth Training
YTP	Youth Training Programme (Northern Ireland)
YTS	Youth Training Scheme

INDEX